The Almost Impregnable Miss Parker

Officer, to the Grand Hotel in the seaside suburb of Muizenburg. It had not yet opened for the summer season and we were billeted there. We all fell into beds provided and I remember I slept till the following morning.

The next day one of the welfare ladies called at the hotel. She was from the committee of 'Bundles for Britain' — a charity which had been collecting clothes for bombed out people in the UK. We were taken to a large warehouse which was stacked with donated clothes. Coats, dresses, suits for men and women hung in rows. Shelves were filled with underwear, blouses, skirts, jerseys, shirts as well as hats and handbags. Everything that someone in our situation might need was there. All were in good condition — there was nothing shabby or well-worn. Some members of the Committee were sorting garments and making them into bundles to be sent to the UK. From this surplus of the charity's store, we were invited to choose what we would like. To have had a bath and to wear clean clothes again helped us all to regain a feeling of normality.

Later in the day Lieutenant Martin came to the hotel. He told us that it was hoped to send us on another ship very soon. Until then we would stay here.

The following days were spent sitting on the beach watching the waves that lapped gently on the sand. The white houses of Muizenburg with the jagged ridge of mountains so close behind — and the warmth of the sun — reminded me of the French Riviera.

THE ALMOST IMPREGNABLE MISS PARKER

Ethel Dallin

ISIS

LARGE PRINT

Oxford

Copyright © Ethel Dallin, 1992

First published in Great Britain 1992
by The Book Guild Ltd.

Published in Large Print 2004 by ISIS Publishing Ltd,
7 Centremead, Osney Mead, Oxford OX2 0ES
by arrangement with
The Book Guild Ltd.

British Library Cataloguing in Publication Data
Dallin, Ethel, 1911–1991
    The almost impregnable Miss Parker. – Large print ed.
    – (Isis reminiscence series)
    1. Dallin, Ethel, 1911–1991
    2. Dallin, Ethel, 1911–1991 – Homes and haunts –
    England – London
    3. Large type books
    4. London (England) – Social life and customs
    – 20th century
    5. London (England) – Biography
    I. Title
    942.1'082'092

ISBN 0–7531–9930–0 (hb)
ISBN 0–7531–9931–9 (pb)

Printed and bound by Antony Rowe, Chippenham

Contents

other extracts — there were many South African men in the Western Desert (More than ever I longed to be in Britain . . . .)

Soon after this Lt. Martin called again. He explained there was a setback for us. Since the weekend when the Orcades was sunk, many more ships had been lost between Durban and Cape Town. Other people were waiting to sail and, with a major offensive in the Middle East, all berths had been commandeered. Our priority was low on the list. Though we must always be ready to fill at a moment's notice, he thought it might be two months before our turn came. In the circumstances the Army would cease paying for our accommodation. The Grand Hotel was nearly booked for the summer season and wanted us to leave.

This was a blow. I was bitterly disappointed and, although she did not say anything to Mr Martin, Ma was worried as she did not know how far her money would stretch. To live on her Army allowance (Mark John's half income), which was now being paid into a Cape Town bank, would be very stringent. A sudden drastic change in her financial situation had happened before in Ma's life — more than once — and now it was happening again. So far our losses from the war in Malaya had been a lesser worry than not having news of her husband — she had felt she could cope once we

It was later discovered that the Assistant Harbour Master in Cape Town was . . . . had been responsible for the sudden shortage of sailings including the Orcades . . . .

PREFACE

Many years ago my husband suggested I translate my bitterness and anger against my mother into words on paper, and then destroy the paper. For days I typed and wept, wept and typed. When I had finished, my husband said "Well done! Now let Emily rest easy in her grave."

But instead of burning those pages I kept them at the bottom of a blanket box and in time added notes about Covent Garden, St Clement Danes, Drury Lane, Ginger Tom and the infamous Cobbler.

Just as secondary cancer began to inhibit even the simplest act of typing, I had the good fortune to meet Wendy Chetwin at St Francis Hospice, Havering, Essex.

Without Wendy and her husband's word processor, my notes would have remained at the bottom of the box until thrown into the dustbin when my old man and I had shuffled off our clogs. And it needed all of Wendy's constant encouragement and occasional chivvying to keep my husband and me from giving up the attempt to make sense of that mass, or mess, of hundreds of accumulated pages.

So I dedicate this book to Wendy and Derek Chetwin for their patience and generosity, to my husband for his love and to the memory of my mother, the indomitable Emily. May she rest easy.

INTRODUCTION

In 1987 I went back to Covent Garden in a wheelchair. Gone were the horses and the sweating, swearing porters. But the cobbles, where I used to run as a skinny kid with one leg of my drawers hanging down, they were still there. Now they jolted my spine and I cursed all the town planners and public authorities who in their stupidity forget the lame, the maimed and the elderly.

Even so, I felt a stir of the old excitement. All those stalls — antique lace instead of white-headed cauliflowers; beads, bangles and baubles instead of golden skinned onions; scarves and gloves of garish hue instead of many fruits and flowers. What a contrast. There was music, there was dancing. And those high prices! The voices were foreign to my ear, still colourful, but different.

There were girls and boys with hair spiked like cockscombs, gaudy as parrots in red, yellow and green. My husband left me briefly while he went to the loo. A youth, uncouth in my eyes with his shaven head and earring dangling from one ear, stopped in front of me.

"This is it," I thought, "I'm going to be mugged." I grasped my handbag tightly and made ready to hit him in the balls with my stick.

"Are you all right?" he asked. "Can I do anything to help?"

"You are very kind," I replied, "but I'm quite all right." How wrong can you get?

Later we were stopped by some Arabian tourists who wanted their pictures taken with a typical English Granny. My husband laughed and I cracked him one with my stick. Then we all began to laugh and I gave in when Americans and Japanese wanted to get in on the act. I wanted to snarl like a tiger but I smiled and pretended to be a demure old lady. Me with my upbringing. For this is where it all started, just a stone's throw away.

CHAPTER ONE

Covent Garden

If you should go to the Drury Lane Theatre, or the Aldwych, or the Waldorf Hotel, or St Clement Danes church, you may notice within that favoured triangle some tenements being tarted up. They may even have their original names — the Stirling and Seddon Buildings.

Although my parents were married at St Clement Danes church, it was not until 1915 that my widowed mother, myself aged four years and my brother moved into Stirling Buildings. I cannot remember much about the 1914-18 war years. If there were shortages of food and clothing, it would have made little difference to us. Shortage of money was our problem. The Armistice I remember only as a vast laughing, cheering and singing crowd in Trafalgar Square, and my mother getting drunk. She became a disgusting stranger to me and for the first time I felt ashamed and betrayed. They were feelings I got to know well.

About a thousand people, including children, lived in the tenements. All were poor, mostly ill-educated if at all, some often drunk and abusive, some not too honest, all struggling to survive in hard times. It was the

1

need to survive that made them into a community. Neighbour spoke to neighbour, neighbour helped neighbour and at times neighbour had a bloody good row with neighbour. Mother was good at all three, particularly the rows. Although not tall, at forty she had a trim upright figure and great physical strength. She was not witty but spoke her mind with devastating directness. When crossed she would unleash an explosive attack that silenced most opposition, for she was afraid of neither man nor devil.

I believe that whatever she knew of love died with my father. Certainly she showed none to me and I have felt that lack for the rest of my life. My brother, two years older than I, fared only slightly better. She always said that she would never marry again even if the man's arse was hung with diamonds. There was no alternative but to turn to work with her strength and dour determination as her only assets. For consolation she turned to alcohol, the chief tranquilliser for the poor at that time. Mother started to drink regularly, but at first only moderately, when we moved into Stirling Buildings.

Our tenement, rent six shillings per week, was on the third floor and consisted of two small rooms, one the bedroom which we all shared, the other the living room and kitchen combined. A sink and a copper were in a small scullery which gave access to the lavatory and coal cupboards. The doors, the floors, the window frames, the picture rails, the fixed dresser, all the woodwork had been treated with creosote. The walls were distempered a dark rust brown colour. It was, you might say, a brown job; if gloom had a colour, this was it. Certain rules had to be obeyed, stairs to be cleaned weekly and so on. One rule said that lino, if you had any, must not reach the skirting boards. This was to prevent the breeding of bed bugs. But bugs being bugs, they continued to procreate and flourish and infested the building from top to bottom.

The centre of our home was the big coal-fired range in our living room. It kept us warm; the oven was excellent for roasting and baking; the top was large and we could heat several cast iron pots and a large kettle all at the same time. There were certain provisos however. First you had to have the coal and for that you had to have the money or a free voucher from the church. Having got your coal, the chimney sometimes got clogged or the wind would blow in the wrong direction; then you ended up with a room full of smoke and soot.

Mother's method of clearing a blocked chimney was dramatic but effective. She would poke up the chimney old clothes soaked in paraffin and then set light to them. There would be a loud bang, the caretaker would be in shock and passers-by in York Street showered in soot. The range also needed to be cleaned with blacklead, this with plenty of spit produced a good polish. The rim and the fire-irons were steel and kept bright with an emery cloth.

Who did the cleaning? Yes, that's right, the range was indeed the centre of my home, the damned thing squatted there always demanding attention or it would sulk and smoke or go out altogether. When the Vicar preached about the "Keeper of the Flame" I imagined some other poor soul stuck with a coal-fired range — not my idea of heaven.

Although I loved the church and the Vicar and his wife, the Pennington Bickfords, many of the sermons were incomprehensible to me. I would struggle with precepts such as "turn the other cheek"; well, I wasn't going to try that for a start! And if "cleanliness is next to godliness" then we had to be high up in His estimation. But why were we afflicted with bed bugs and what was their part in the Almighty plan? Everyone in the tenements was fanatically clean, forever scrubbing and washing. My theory is that all that washing, coppers always on the boil, clothes steaming in front of the range, actually promoted the breeding of bed bugs. The continually damp warm environment with all that food, our flesh, must have been their idea of heaven. We waged constant war on them, burnt them alive with lighted candles, doused them in paraffin, stabbed them with hat pins, but still they multiplied, coming out for their nightly fix of blood. A bed bug is flat, dark brown and round, which when alive has a distinct odour but when dead, whether squashed, pierced or fried, gives off a stench that is uniquely revolting.

Good Friday was ordained by Mother to be the Grand Bug Hunting Day. The pictures would be taken down and the frames treated with paraffin, the paper backings burnt and replaced with new, the bugs trying to escape stabbed with hat pins. All our furniture, the table, the chairs, the beds, the floors, the doors, the window frames, anything made of wood was given the same treatment. The excitement of hunting the bed bug probably does not compare with chasing the fox and "gotcher, you bugger" has not the same ring as "tally ho" or whatever it is those gallant gentlemen in red coats cry at the death of a fox, but I think that the primitive blood-lust, the desire to kill was the same.

At the end of the day, our aggression slaked with socially justifiable slaughter, and despite the appalling stench, we would celebrate with stew and dumplings. But it was only a battle, the war was never won.

The weekly hunt for lice in my hair was not all that thrilling. It was a tedious ritual of combing out the nits with a steel fine-toothed comb and a wash in a solution made from Quassia chips. This was followed by an all over scrub down in a zinc bath. Despite our lack of space, decency was preserved for I never saw my brother or mother naked. Keatings Powder was also used against fleas and lice and some childrens' heads were liberally dusted with it, much to their chagrin. I was at least spared that, although my long hair made nits harder to get at and I hated the regular mauling by the visiting school nurse with its implication of being unclean. It was no consolation that the rest of the class were treated the same. Almost all of us came from the same or similar tenements anyway, so I had no real reason for complaint.

Ours was a church school and there is a saying "as poor as a church mouse", but the mice were probably fatter than we were and the church became a refuge and a place of joy to me.

As a family we went to every Sunday evening service, mainly to be seen as "the decent poor", to be deserving of the occasional five shilling grocery voucher and a ticket for fourteen pounds of coal and perhaps a small hamper at Christmas. The Vicar, the Reverend Pennington Bickford, and his wife were a wonderful couple and probably knew that our Sunday clothes spent the rest of the week in pawn. I, being innocently unaware of any mercenary motives, would enter the church with true feelings of reverence and childlike wonder.

To me it was a really beautiful church. It had a high arched ceiling decorated in dark blue with gold stars and cherubs. Around three sides of the church was a gallery which was often fully occupied. The choir stalls were large with a space in front for a small orchestra. On the left there was a special shrine, ornately carved, always gay with flowers, known as the Flower Sellers Shrine. This was another of Mrs Bickford's inspirations and a token of her care and affection for her "gels", the flower sellers.

Some of these "gels" were quite old "gels", but they would go along early in the morning to the market with their large wicker baskets, buy their flowers, bring them back to the tenements and make up posies. Then with their wicker baskets they would go along to Piccadilly Circus to sell to the wealthy ladies and their gents. In the winter the posies would often be violets and the hands that held them covered with chilblains.

The old parish hall, which survived the wholesale slum clearance of the area known as Clare Market, was very spartan inside with rough wooden tables and forms, but was another centre of Mrs Bickford's care. She would purchase wholesale rolls of red flannel and white calico and sell them at cost price to the "Mothers Meetings". There the women would be able to make flannel vests and petticoats and calico sheets. The white calico was also used to make huge drawers the women wore under their long skirts.

Mother had the good sense to buy a Singer sewing machine which, at one shilling a week, took years to pay for, but it paid for itself over and over again, for I was still using it sixty years later and regret having parted with it.

Mrs Bickford also made sure that in winter free hot soup and pieces of bread were provided. We were hungry but we didn't starve. These Mothers Meetings were lively centres of gossip and rough good-humoured banter and I realize more than ever that our community was like a "London Village" of the poor, which was at the heart of another world, one of wealth, privilege and power. To me it was the very hub about which the rest of the world revolved.

Another of Mrs Bickford's inspirations was the revival of the beating of the bounds of St Clement Danes parish in 1920. I was nine years old and among those chosen as I was in the church choir. We were told the history of the boundary plaques, that the ceremony may have originated in Roman times. On the day itself we donned our cassocks and surplices and were each given a long willow wand. We marched round to each of the plaques in turn and took great pleasure in giving them a good thrashing while the vicar said a prayer. I irreverently thought of mother invoking the Lord while giving me a good hiding and whenever possible gave the plaques an extra swipe just for me. We had to go in small rowing boats to beat the plaques on the Thames side of the Embankment, quite an adventure in itself.

Mrs Bickford also revived the old "Oranges and Lemons" service. We were taught to play the rhyme on hand bells while the church bells rang out. We also took part in reading the Lessons, recited the rhyme and finally were rewarded with oranges and lemons piled on tables in the porch as we filed out. I don't know if the fruit was given free by the traders in the market, but knowing Mrs Bickford's persuasive powers, I shouldn't be surprised. As this was the first revival for many years it was quite an occasion and was broadcast live by the BBC at Savoy Hill.

The Vicar and his curate made regular visits to the tenements to remind the sinners that they could be saved. For most of the sinners their salvation lay at the bottom of a pint glass in the public bar of *The Falstaff* opposite Drury Lane Theatre. This the vicar knew and they knew that he knew, but courtesy prevailed on both sides. After all the Reverend Gent was only doing his job. And they had theirs to do, poorly paid manual jobs mostly, hard work, long hours, with no pension to hang their hats on at the end of it all. They worked as porters in the market, barmen and barmaids in the pubs, hotels and clubs, cleaners, dressers, scene-shifters and doormen in the theatres.

Work, noise and drinking went on almost non-stop, starting at two o'clock in the morning with the gang of men from Westminster City Council hosing down and sweeping the streets. In the gaslight they looked theatrical and unreal in their wide waterproof hats, tunics and rubber thigh boots. They carried the hose in a red hand cart and the hose with its polished brass nozzle would be attached to a water hydrant. On the occasions that I watched, the man with the hose had a wonderful time, sending the jet high in the air, making a curtain of water as high as a house, then with a flick of his wrist making it collapse. They were a noisy lot as well, hard luck for light sleepers, which we were not. Noise was part of our background, only noticed when absent.

Covent Garden itself was full of chaotic life and noise from about three in the morning with the rattle and clatter of hooves and iron rims on cobbles, costermongers grumbling and cursing as they jostled their carts through the narrow gas-lit streets to get the best positions for loading up. All the pubs in the market had a special licence to open early and did a thriving trade in breakfasts, beer, rum and coffee. By midday the bartering and shouting died away. But the drinking went on for other pubs had been open from mid-morning.

"What is truth?" asked Pontius Pilate before pushing off. My truth is not an historical one, but a personal idiosyncratic one. Events overlap and memories contradict one another. Was it noisy all the time? Memory says "Yes", reason replies "Surely not", but before the clamour of the market had ended, the everyday traffic and trade had started up. Deliveries of food, alcohol and linen were made to the Waldorf Hotel. Sometimes great blocks of ice were man-handled from a lorry and down the stairs into the kitchen. Similar deliveries were made to the theatres, but there were also actors coming and going to dress rehearsals or matinees. There were coalmen, fishmongers and even greengrocers making their rounds of the tenements. There were street musicians and acrobats. There was always a barrel-organ with a sad-eyed monkey in a red coat perched on top. Tenants would be out at work at all hours, probably with a stop at the pub both going and coming back. Kids out from school raced up and down the stairs, skipping, playing release or marbles. When the gas lighter came to turn on the street lamps with his magic pole, a little procession would follow him with "How's it done, mister? Where d'ya keep your matches then?"

In the evenings the gentlemen and their ladies would arrive at the theatres in their Rolls and their Daimlers. The chauffeurs in polished gaiters and uniforms matching the colour of their cars were always very formal and correct; a discreet incline of the head, a touch to the cap as they opened the door for their passengers. The gentlemen would be in full evening dress and capes with silk linings. The ladies wore gowns of satin or velvet with sequins and pearls and a corsage of flowers and a fur stole around their shoulders. If it was raining the attendants in their bright livery would be ready with umbrellas to escort the patrons into the foyer, which would be all gilt and crimson and decorated with flowers. Attendants would pocket their tips with the speed of conjurors.

We kids would go along to observe, but also to weigh up the worth of the audience. We would work in teams of two or three, one team for Drury Lane, one for the Aldwych, one for the Strand and one for the Gaiety, and so on. We would meet up and discuss possibilities. Then back to the theatres in time for the interval, for the gentlemen would stroll out to smoke their cigars and the ladies would stroll out too, elegant and relaxed. Picking out the kindest face, we would ask so politely if the face wanted its chocolate box. This often worked. The boxes would be discarded later in a side street, but any chocolates put into a bag. I once had a whole bottom layer. Then back to the tenements for the share out and the feast. They don't make chocolates like that any more!

The cars would be parked in the same streets as those used by the horse and donkey carts in the morning. Each chauffeur had been given a numbered card. The attendants would call out the number when the white shirt fronts and their ladies were ready to go home or on to a restaurant. Some restaurants remained open until one or two in the morning.

Soon the street cleaners would be back at work again. Perhaps there was a short period of silence, broken only by the tread of the bobbies' feet on patrol from Bow Street, but I wouldn't swear to it.

In our gang was my best friend Maud Buchan. She was small, plain and quite solemn; but when she laughed her whole face would light up as if the sun shone just for her. She was the youngest of a large family who rented two tenements and she had to run the errands for, and clear up after, her elders. We were the same age and had much in common especially our grievances. I would complain about my dragon of a mother and she her tyrant of a father.

He was a skinny man with cropped black hair and eyes set deep in a pale face. He was always ready with an oath or a backhander for anyone who dared interrupt his work. This he did at home in a small room empty but for his bench, his tools and his jugs of beer. He was a highly skilled surgical shoe and boot maker and never seemed to use patterns. I was astonished that such beautiful work could be made from instructions written on tatty pieces of paper or cardboard.

When a pair of boots or shoes were ready, it was Maud's job to take them to the main workshop in Bloomsbury. It was quite a distance and I normally went with her. This happened two or three times a week, about six o'clock in the evening. Mr Buchan would be away to the pub in a vile temper as usual, to return later stupefied or in a sullen rage. Mrs Buchan must have spent those evenings in fear, but we would be off, carefree, especially in fine weather, round the corner into Drury Lane.

The shoes would be in a heavy cloth drawstring bag over Maud's shoulder. We would gawp in at the stage door of the theatre, plaguing everyone with questions until we were told to get out. We would polish our noses on the windows of the food shops, especially the butchers where they were cooking faggots and pigs trotters. At the top of Drury Lane was a German bakers, Isaac's the fishmonger and also the first Sainsbury's store. The German baker disappeared without trace, but Isaac's became known throughout London, and everyone in the country must know of Sainsbury's.

At Southampton Row we would cross over New Oxford Street into Russell Square, past the British Museum to an old house that must have been very fine in its time. It had an air of battered grandeur. In the basement were several men still making shoes and boots. Maud had been told what money to ask for, to collect the materials for the next job and not to hang about. There were no invoices and no questions asked; and so began our first adventure into crime.

We were then nine years old and apart from the odd nicking of an apple or an orange were previously of "good character". At least I think we were. Looking at a pair of exquisitely made boots I suggested that we should ask for a little extra. Maud was horrified and terrified, but finally agreed providing I did the asking. With my knees clamped firmly together to prevent me from wetting my knickers, I calmly added an extra sixpence to the price and got it. We walked sedately for a few yards and then ran to the nearest saveloy and pease pudding shop. This gave me something else to think about at church on Sunday, but it didn't stop me asking for an extra shilling next time. I dare not go above that and we always gave Mrs Buchan at least fourpence. We would not tell her the whole story, but said we had earned it running errands, which was the truth, wasn't it?

Luckily we were never found out, for Maud would have been beaten black and blue by her father. He wouldn't have touched me, Mother would have seen to that; but my punishment would have been just as severe, Mother would have seen to that too. Mrs Buchan would not have escaped either. The poor sickly woman usually had a black eye at the best of times. For our misdeeds she would have suffered an appalling beating. What strange webs we weave when we practice to deceive. Was right done by doing wrong? Did the bully and the boss deserve to lose that shilling? And were we wrong to benefit from it? How now, Pontius Pilate?

Maud was very reticent about her eighteen year old sister Betsy whose ways were mysterious. She worked at Odhams the printers. In the morning she would go out pale, plain, dowdy and silent. But after work, when she went out in the evening she was transformed utterly. On her head a flat black Spanish type hat with a red rose for decoration, her jet black hair at shoulder length and her pale face dramatized by orange lipstick. In a well-fitting, good quality dress or coat with matching handbag and gloves, thin stockings and high heeled shoes she would step out without a backward glance and without a word to anyone. What time she came home I don't know, for I never saw her although I rarely got to bed before eleven at night. But there she would be next morning, plain, dowdy, silent on her way to work.

By now my life had some sort of routine and rhythm, starting at six a.m. on a weekday with the clamour of our postman's alarm clock. Mother made sure that we were up, dressed and properly admonished before she set off to clean the offices and light the fires at the Exchequer and Audit Department on the Embankment at Blackfriars. She did this whatever the season and whatever the weather, whether she felt ill or well.

The wind slicing across the river on a winter's morning was enough to rattle the teeth of a corpse in a coffin. Even worse were the peasouper fogs. Sinister, thick, acrid and yellow, the fog would bring London almost to a stop. The mournful warnings of the boats on the river, the shrill of the policeman's whistle, or the stamp of a horse's hoof in the next street were muffled, distorted, ominous. Most people felt apprehensive; accidents and broken bones were frequent. Some sufferers with chest complaints were literally killed by the fog. There would be the usual knowing nods and talk of "pneumonia, the old man's friend" and "he or she is best out of it all". But it seemed that no matter how wretchedly you had lived, you had to have a good send off at the end.

A pauper's grave was the final humiliation after a life of poverty. Insurance policies were only a few pence a week, and the agents were for ever urging people to increase their cover for "when the times comes."

The funerals were grand affairs. Tall black horses with flowing manes and tails and with fine velvet back cloths would draw the black hearse. The coffin and the hearse would be covered with flowers. The horses were trained to walk proudly, necks curved, the splendid black plumes on their heads dipping and swaying as if in homage to the dead. There would be at least two carriages behind to carry the chief mourners; others would have to walk. When it rained streaks of black dye could cause embarrassment.

After the church service, the burial was usually at places like Highgate Cemetery. My father was buried there as was Karl Marx. Sometimes on the way the cortege would stop at a convenient pub and everyone would nip in for a quick one in memory of the departed. After the funeral, back at the tenements, there would be high tea and several more quick or not so quick ones. The dead would be praised fulsomely. "Poor old cow, she did her best" or "He was a miserable old sod, but God rest him anyway". The whole thing would often end in bitter recriminations and a punch up. And everyone went home happy.

But back to my routine. Whatever the weather, whatever the season, whether ill or well, I would be off to the Market. I never tired of the place. Every day was newly minted, always promising adventure. After breakfast of bread and margarine, or bread with vile tasting cocoa butter, it also promised an apple, an orange, a pear; anything I could scrounge. Sometimes I would forget to ask and help myself, but everyone was either too busy to notice, or turned a blind eye. I on the contrary was always on the alert, alive to every sensation. Horses' hooves striking sparks from cobbles, the rattle of iron rimmed wheels, the shouts and fights of the porters, the smell of leather, dung and sweat, of fruit, vegetables and flowers; the sheer explosive energy of it all.

The porters wore dark old jackets or waistcoats with corduroy trousers tied at the ankle or knee with string and thick heavy boots. They wore flat caps on which they placed pads of felt so that they could carry on their heads round wicker baskets, stacked one upon another, of fruit — cherries, apples, gooseberries, plums, pears.

The porters had to be skilful and strong and were rightly proud of their ability. The more baskets they could carry (the average was seven or eight) and the faster they worked, the more they earned. It should have been set to music, a ballet of baskets weaving and swaying as the porters moved swiftly round one another and between sellers and buyers, dodging the barrows loaded high with sacks of peas, beans, potatoes, cabbages, carrots, boxes of oranges, lemons, grapefruit, trays of tomatoes and soft fruit, strawberries, raspberries.

The scene changed from season to season. Seventy years ago frozen vegetables were unknown. When peas came on to the market, the buyers from the restaurants and clubs would place orders day by day for shelled peas. One merchant specialized in these and employed local women from seven in the morning to do the shelling. They were usually old hands at the job and, in their wide brimmed flat straw hats and large white aprons, would arrive with their own chairs and sit themselves round in a circle. Each was given a bag of peas and a bowl and these would be filled, emptied and

17

filled over and over again. Each sheller had her tally and urged the others on with banter and laughter.

It was a grand way to spend a summer morning, with plenty of cups of tea from the stall at the back of St Paul's Church.

With the mists of autumn and as the mornings became dark and cold with approaching winter, shapes and shadows shifted and changed under the gas lamps and the lights from the stalls and shop windows. The superb glass roof of the Floral Hall glowed from within with a new splendour. The hundreds of candle lamps on the carts converged from all the side streets towards the centre. I would not have been surprised to see imps and goblins somersaulting along the pavements. I was quite sure they were there anyway. Mr Jones assured me that his grandmother kept one in an empty whisky bottle and let him out at Christmas as a treat.

The market at Christmas time was hyperactive, supply barely able to cope with demand. The shops were piled high with fruit, particularly the stands selling tangerines. Figs and dates did a brisk trade. Mistletoe, holly and Christmas trees hung from roof beams and filled every spare corner. Bags of walnuts, brazils, almonds and cobnuts lay open for inspection. Bowler hatted buyers from the hotels pushed their way through the crowds to buy the best of everything, especially the large trees. They would join the porters for rum and coffee and more than a few were overflowing with good cheer by eight a.m. It was a good time for free samples and the extra penny or sixpence.

For a week after Christmas trade was sluggish, the air of goodwill grown cold, but in the Central Avenue there was a special smell of pineapples, grapes and melons. My first pineapple was a half rotten one thrown to me by one of the brown-coated traders. I drooled over the sweet, sharp taste of it. The juice ran through my fingers, down my chin and on to my frock and I proudly reeked of pineapple all through the morning class at school. I got a clout on the ear at dinner time, of course, as Mother was at home between jobs.

However the Floral Hall was my particular joy, for I had made a friend there. He was tall, red haired, blue eyed and ugly. Wounds of war had scarred his face into a permanent scowl. As he walked he would lurch as if about to swoop. He frightened and fascinated me, so ugly among so much beauty.

But one Ascension Day, when I was about six or seven, we had been asked to take flowers for the special service. All I had was twopence. Cap (everyone called him that) had several boxes of gorgeous red roses. I looked and looked and looked. Suddenly he swooped towards me and harshly demanded to know what I wanted. I started so violently that one leg of my drawers came down and I babbled on about Ascension Day, St Clement Danes, and my twopence and could I have some roses please sir! He looked down at me in astonishment, lurched about a couple of times, told someone else to shut their gob, then picked up a handful of roses, wrapped them in paper and thrust them into my hands. I stammered out my thanks and turned to go, but one great hand grabbed me.

"Twopence," he growled.

However, next day, when I took a couple of rolls I had nicked from the back of the Waldorf, and explained how Mrs Bickford was so pleased with the roses, he gave me my twopence back. Mind you he never gave me any more flowers, but I went to see him every day he was there and sometimes he would send me to one of the stalls for a cup of tea and a sandwich which we would share.

One day I was terrified when Mother turned up. She stood and glared at Cap. Cap glared back. Not a single word passed between them. Then with a "Behave yourself!" to me, mother turned away.

"That your Mum?" asked Cap.

"Yes," I said.

"Hard luck," was his reply and never mentioned her again.

He was in pain most of the time and this made him short tempered and quarrelsome. More than once I saw him send another man reeling with a terrible blow to the chest.

It must have been during the very next winter that he got into a brawl with several men at once. He knocked out two, suffered a broken nose himself and ended up fighting three policemen. They eventually carted him off to Bow Street police station in a hooded long basket-type chair. I sobbed out my tale to mother.

"The poor sod," she said and put her arm round my shoulder.

It was such a rare gesture of compassion that I cried the more in gratitude. I never saw or spoke of Cap again and avoided the Floral Market for some time.

The winter was a hard time for everyone, especially the horses, for they often slipped on the icy cobbles. Down they would go, perhaps breaking a shaft, which would dig into a hind leg. Once a horse broke its leg; I shall never forget the screams. The other horses reared and kicked. Men were shouting advice and cursing each other. All was chaos until a vet shot the poor beast. The head thudded back, the eyes rolled red and I was sick.

Apart from differences in size and colour each horse and donkey had a distinct personality of its own. Some were obviously old, wearily trying to rest first one limb then another, heads drooping from scrawny necks. Some were well turned out, others had harness tied together with string. What I know of horses I learned from Mr John Jones, High Class Fruiterer and Greengrocer of Lambeth, whose name and credentials were spelt out in golden letters on the side of his smart green van. I also learnt straight from the horses' mouth. I was in Maiden Lane and wearing a multi-coloured woollen hat with a pompom on top. A horse whipped this off my head, dropped it, stamped on it and then peed on it! There was a lot of laughter and I went hot with embarrassment and rage. I hit what I could reach of the horse and was about to kick him when Mr Jones, Fruiterer and Greengrocer of Lambeth, restrained me.

"I shouldn't do that, Missie," he said in a soft Welsh accent. "And you should look where you're going, you know!"

"Look where I'm going!" I shouted. "Look where I'm going! I was on the pavement! My mum's going to kill me! That hat was worth, er, was worth two shillings!"

"Little girls shouldn't tell lies," said Mr Jones calmly. "I might come up from the country and sell cabbages, but I'm not that green. See now, here's a bob, that should do."

It so happened I was pleased to see the back of that rotten hat and got a better one from jumble for threepence.

But next day Mr Jones and I had more words. There in Wellington Street was his horse peeing all over the pavement. Other horses did this often enough, but I was full of righteous indignation and called Mr Jones's horse an ugly, brown, disgusting brute. Mr Jones was not impressed. One thing led to another, that horses were not just brown but roan or bay or chestnut or sorrel and that Cobbler was as fine a chestnut as you would see this side of Wales.

Mr Jones in his lilting voice told me about pit ponies, of horses lugging guns through the mud at Flanders where he was, to use his words, "a greasy gunner". He was sick of both the war and the pits. With money borrowed from his mother-in-law he had leased a small shop in Lambeth. He and his wife were happy enough and thought Londoners were not clever, just crafty.

It still rankled that he had been caught when buying his first horse. It was black, strong, sound in wind and limb and cheap.

"I should have known," said John Jones sadly. "He went like a dream until Westminster Bridge, then he bolted. His mouth was like iron. A wonder he didn't kill us both. Took the skin off my hands he did. Bolted again next morning. I sold him in the afternoon. Made a small profit, mind you."

Cobbler was a rogue, a show off, a thief, but he was tough and willing to pull a full load twelve or even fourteen hours a day.

"He's got bottom," said Mr Jones, leaning up against Cobbler while the three of us munched apples. "Bottom" it seemed was a word of praise, it meant staying power. Mr Jones straightened up and Cobbler nearly fell over.

"See that," said Mr Jones affectionately, "the cheeky bugger was leaning on me!"

Then there was the case of the policeman's helmet. Cobbler was minding his own business for a change, happy with a full nose-bag of chaff and oats.

"Fine animal," said the policeman, patting Cobbler's neck. The next moment he staggered back clutching his head as Cobbler coshed him with his nose-bag. The helmet rolled into the wet and pungent gutter. Mr Jones's face went white with shock and disbelief. A guffaw of laughter echoed down the street. The policeman was also Welsh which seemed to make matters worse. In a voice that was neither soft nor lilting, he made clear that he had every intention of putting both Mr Jones and Cobbler behind bars. He snatched his stained helmet from Mr Jones and stalked off in the direction of Bow Street.

Mr Jones threatened Cobbler with awful retribution and I ran off, choking with laughter. I called back "Don't forget he's got bottom!" and convulsed with my own wit. "Oh what a lot of bottom he's got!"

Even Mother laughed when I told her the tale.

Apparently she had had quite a morning herself. Having finished at Blackfriars by nine o'clock, she went as usual to the Inns of Court opposite Lincolns Inn Fields, to clean barristers' apartments. She swept the rooms, scrubbed the kitchen floors and the stairs. This morning a large rat ran over her hand, then turned and faced her eyeball to eyeball. Mother fell over her bucket and down the stairs. Although she was winded and her skirt was soaked, she finished the job, but was going to give notice on Friday.

"Mum, you can't do that! It's one of your best jobs," I exclaimed. "And where's your staying power?"

As she was trusted by the chef, Mum had the pick of the leftovers from dinners and banquets and you don't turn your back on food. Even a bag of cooked quail, though no bigger than sparrows, is better than nothing. I should have kept my mouth shut for Mother promptly gave me a bundle of laundry to iron.

Mother really disliked this particular customer. She was a bit lah-de-da and her underwear fine and dainty with frills and lace. More than once, sloshing the clothes about furiously, Mother would vow that this was the last time. She hadn't the patience to wash and iron "fancy rubbish". But the ironing was given to me, for I had learnt to iron by the time I was eight.

Preparing the iron was a job in itself. First it had to be heated on the range; if spit ran off the sole quickly it was hot enough. Then the sole had to be polished with soap and emery paper and buffed until it was spotless. A piece of blanket from the printing works made a fine ironing cover for the table. In order to reach I had to kneel on a chair, the iron was heavy and I had to be very careful not to scorch anything. I also did the pricing for fancy wear and would price it item by item, always putting the pot on, an extra threepence for this or sixpence for that, but the lady always paid up. The result was always the same. Mother and the money ended up in the pubs. God, how I hated the pubs.

I had become numerate almost before I had become literate. Basically food, money and beer were the main preoccupations of my childhood. If I hadn't known the colour of Covent Garden, the glamour of theatreland and the West End, the pomp and majesty of Westminster, the wonderful liberating freedom of the Royal Parks and the support of St Clement Danes, my life would have been a miserable drudgery. There was the companionship of the tenements, that is true. It is also true that although everyone knew one another, it didn't automatically follow that you liked one another.

For instance, I detested my brother. He never did his share of the work and I was punished for his misdemeanours as well as my own. Directly below us lived Miss McCarthy and her brother. Every time Bill and I fought blow for blow, kicking, scratching, biting, the vibrations would break the McCarthy's gas mantles. Miss McCarthy would catch Mother on the stairs to complain. Mother would suggest that the McCarthy's move to another address, preferably as far away as possible. But I got clumped just the same.

After some years Miss McCarthy and I became friends, though Mother remained resolutely hostile. I always thought of the brother as the little man in the bowler hat, the downtrodden clerk with the shiny-arsed trousers. He was ever so polite, perpetually anxious. Worse off than we were, they were both too shy or too proud to borrow or ask for help. They were so respectable!

One evening I knocked on their door with a few flowers which Miss McCarthy received with a hushed "thank you" and looked as if she were going to cry. She invited me in and there they were with one boiled egg between them! She took a little of the yolk on her bread and her brother had the rest. I felt close to tears myself and made an embarrassed exit. We were rich in comparison!

Often our clothes were a lot of old jumble with a few cast offs from the theatres. Sometimes I went to school not knowing whether I was the Fairy Queen or the Principal Boy. But some of our neighbours worked at the Savoy Hotel as waiters and waitresses and whenever the Savoy had a change of crockery or cutlery so did we.

Mother often brought home leftovers from her various jobs, and for sixpence you could buy a one pound block of dripping with lovely thick jelly at the base. We would scoop off the jelly and barter the rest for vegetables or whatever. Then there were giblets from the poulterers in Soho. It was quite a long walk but I enjoyed going.

Soho was both frightening and exciting; a venture into foreign territory with its narrow streets busy with strange people, the most conspicuous but the most withdrawn being the Chinese. Not so some of the women with their strutting ways, bright clothes and vivid faces. I thought that these must be stage people of a sort. They certainly put on an act. It was many years later that I realized some of them at least must have been prostitutes. It seems hard to believe, given my background, how ignorant and naïve I remained about sex and I have no lurid tales of being molested in any way. Perhaps it was my very innocence that spared me from such unpleasant incidents. In Soho itself the traders seemed more aggressive, almost ready to sandbag customers into buying, particularly in Berwick Market. I lingered only to take a deep smell at a baker's shop with loaves, rolls, cakes and pastries of every conceivable sort which could not be bought elsewhere.

Coming home with a large shopping bag full of giblets was a bit harder. I would change the bag from one hand to another and stop every now and again for a breather. I remember thinking "What I need is more Cobbler's bottom!" I had a fit of the giggles and people gave me a few queer looks. This provoked me all the more and I ended up with the hiccups. The giblets cost sixpence and were delicious made into a pie, using dripping for the crust. Even better were the fried livers.

Looking back it seems as if life was either feast or famine. Hunger, it is said, is the best sauce for a meal, but we should never have gone hungry if it were not for the pubs. How I hated the pubs!

I loathed drunkenness, the stupidities, the false cheerfulness and euphoria. I felt angry and bitter with Mother, the awful waste, that she should toil every day from six a.m. until seven thirty p.m. and spend most of what she earned on beer. More than she earned, for I worked too, scrubbing steps, washing and ironing clothes, but I was not paid. More than she earned, because any decent clothes, her wedding ring, anything of value was in and out of pawn. We owed money to tally men with their smarmy ways, forever keeping us in debt, and finally the most soul-destroying, crippling experience of all — the money lenders. Most people are familiar with the old rhyme:

> "Up and down the City Road,
> In and out the Eagle.
> That's the way the money goes,
> Pop goes the Weasel!
> Half a pound of tuppenny rice,
> Half a pound of treacle.
> That's the way the money goes,
> Pop goes the Weasel!"

I am uncertain of the word "Weasel"; I believe it was a slang expression for hat, but the rhyme jocularly captures the truth of the matter. Every Monday morning Mother made time in between jobs to take the tram to City Road, Clerkenwell, to visit Uncle, as the pawnbroker was known. Although she begrudged the tram fare, it was better than having one's linen, clean linen in this case, on display at the local pop shop.

At City Road the shop was very dark inside with six cubicles. In the gloom you would wait until it was your turn with Uncle. With his white beard, he seemed old and frail, but he was impervious to tears or tantrums. Very rarely did he budge from his price. "I'm doing you a favour, lady," he would say. Then, of course, there was the interest to pay on those items not redeemed, like her wedding ring which remained as good as new in Uncle's care. There wasn't much time to argue anyway for the rent man was due at twelve thirty and had to be paid whoever else went short.

Mother did not often resort to the tally men. They sold mostly bed linen or clothing on weekly credit, and the debt and payments were entered on a tally card. If a pair of sheets cost ten shillings you could pop them for six shillings, showing an immediate gain, and to hell with what happened next week. Once again Mother avoided the scrutiny of neighbours by going to Dawson's, a large department store in City Road which accepted Provident cheques. It was a similar arrangement, you would buy a cheque for ten shillings, pay back at one shilling per week plus interest, but Mother could go straight from Dawson's to Uncle's and none would be wiser except those to whom she owed the money.

I have thought about this so often. Mother and her cronies were uneducated but not unintelligent, yet they had this curious blend of fatalism, "what is to be will be" and optimism, "something will turn up". Sometimes they were only too right, they turned up in court, or their toes turned up in a coffin. They, or I should say we, were born losers; the winners were the publicans and the money lenders. The questions posed by the Church — Why are we here? What is life for? Is it worth it? What is truth? (Good old Pilate) — were all abstractions and the answers, at best, remote. Questions like "Where is the rent and the next meal coming from?" required immediate and practical solutions. The pop shop postponed the day of reckoning and in the pub you could forget it.

I find this difficult to write about, but I may as well get it down and out of the way. Bitterness, anger, disgust, loathing, these are the words I associate with pubs. Those that I remember most clearly were *The Falstaff* and *The Globe* opposite Drury Lane Theatre in Catherine Street. *The King's Head* on the corner of Russell Street, *The Marlborough Head* in Drury Lane and *The Princess* in Long Acre. All were within staggering distance of each other.

The first four were strictly spit and sawdust pubs. Sawdust or a mixture of sawdust and sand was on the floors to soak up the spilt beer, the urine and the vomit. Spittoons were there for those able to aim straight. In the "public" there was a brass rail running the length of the bar and about a foot from the floor and a wooden table and bench. No darts, no dominoes, no shove ha'penny, no piano. The saloon, a little better furnished with a couple of cast iron tables and hard backed chairs, was little used. The urinal and lavatory were always at the back and were quite foul. Many of the customers preferred to use the gutters. One of these was Windy Winnie who would stand with one foot on the pavement, the other in the road, to pee and fart prodigiously.

These pubs were always crowded despite the conditions. Under the gas lamps, the heat and smoke filled air was suffocating; the reek of stale beer, cheap tobacco and the stink of sweat was nauseating; the noise an overwhelming cacophony of shouts and raucous laughter.

From the age of seven or eight, at about ten o'clock at night, my friends having gone to bed, I went miserably from one pub to another looking for Mother. Having found her I had to wait until it was safe to wriggle my way through the crowd to remind her that the gas lamps on the stairs of the tenements were turned out promptly at eleven. Normally she was in a cheerful stupor and came without a row. I would guide her home praying that she would not vomit or lose control of her bladder, or worse. Back at the tenements I had to remove her skirt and filthy shoes and get her into bed. If we did not make it by eleven there was the additional hazard of the pitch black stairs and the stray drunk sprawled out on one of the landings.

On Saturday we rarely made it before lights out. The police would caution us as they picked up their regulars from the gutters and pushed them without ceremony into the unlit hallways. Those that resisted ended up in the cells at Bow Street.

I once tried to explain to a priest in Little Venice my inadequacy as a Christian, my inability to forgive my mother, but my fear of losing her. I was then about fourteen or fifteen. His tired old eyes set in a face incredibly crumpled and crevassed by time smiled at me.

"Tell me," he said.

I fudged and fumbled. The best I could manage was "I'm too much of a sinner, Father." He waved a hand towards the church.

"No problem, my child, we are all sinners here."

The attraction was very strong to participate in a group joined together by a common experience, the need for verbal and physical contact, the affirmation of being human. I am expressing this so badly, but I think that it was Mother's need to be with others of her own kind, the need of a social life that required neither pretence or pretension, that first drew her to the pubs. And, of course, she could justify her drinking. "Beer is good for you," the advertisements said so. It was a food, it helped you to sleep, it was a laxative, a diuretic, better than any medicine. Was not our own doctor half-cut most of the time? Beer, beer, glorious beer, fill yourself right up to here! After the first glass or two of porter, troubles and inhibitions were forgotten, argument became lively, laughter louder, more infectious and even if the fights were more frequent as the quarrelsome became aggressive, it all added to the spectacle. What did it matter what was said? They were communicating; they belonged. I was on the outside and did not belong.

There were moments of comedy. One humid night I came back downstairs for some fresh air and a good cry. A cab drew up and Ginger Tom fell out. Now Tom was ginger, short, thick-set with china blue eyes, a fresh complexion and a cheerful "watcher, mate" for everyone. His nickname was due less to his colour than to his success with the ladies, about which at the time I knew nothing. With a seraphic smile Tom embraced the nearest lamp post and slid gracefully to the ground. The cabbie was not amused.

"Ethel, me old love," called Tom, "Sort this lot out for me, will yer?" He produced a handful of coins.

"Two bob," said the driver.

"Half a crown," said Tom.

"Blimey, you *are* drunk!" I said as the cab rattled away.

"Yer right, Ethel, yer so bloody right." He pulled himself up by the lamp post. "And when I'm drunk I've a weakness for policemen's helmets. The police don't like it. The magistrate don't like it. Me wife don't like it. So I take a cab from the pub and everybody's 'appy!"

A voice from behind said, "I'm not bloody happy, you scruff!"

It was Mrs Tom, a thin wisp of a woman who worked as a dresser at the Aldwych Theatre. She belted Tom round the ear. He promptly sat down again.

"Hello Duchess, come to give me a 'and, 'ave yer?" The duchess intimated that she had castration in mind, but the purpose of cutting his balls off was lost on me. Together we hoisted Tom to his feet again. The duchess had a candle and as we lurched uncertainly up the stairs, our shadows dancing on the walls, she said,

"You're a good kid. See you tomorrow."

Feeling much better I went back to bed.

Tom's wife's name was Ivy and whereas I usually called adults by their surname, it was not so with these two. Mother had tartly christened them Ginger Tom and Clinging Ivy, but whatever the truth of Tom's reputation, Ivy did not cling, she clouted. Tom never retaliated although he had arms like a gorilla. He would lift her up, kiss her and say,

"Steady on, Duchess." I am convinced that they were genuinely fond of each other and that this made Mother jealous.

Ivy was very happy at the Aldwych and would tell me the latest chat about Tom Walls, Robertson Hare, Ralph Lynn and Mary Brough. She was fond of them all as were most of us kids, for they were generous with their pennies. When Tom Walls's horse, April the Fifth, won the Derby, there was much jubilation for most of the locals had backed it.

Mary Brough was my favourite. She was a lovely person and would have made a smashing mum. For years she appeared in the advertisements for Robin Starch. I never understood why she always arrived at the theatre on foot when the others came by car. According to Ivy, Mary was afraid of cars and came by tram, insisting on sitting in the middle. At the bottom of Savoy Hill she would get out and walk the rest of the way.

The Ben Travers farces, *Cuckoo in the Nest*, *Rookery Nook*, *Tons of Money*, for example, seemed to run and run. During one of them, almost on the stroke of nine, the audience were shaken by a bang that could be heard in the streets outside. Ivy used to say, "That made the buggers jump!"

The shows at the Strand were not always as popular as those at the Aldwych and Drury Lane so sometimes my friend Maud and I were given tickets by those changing their minds at the last moment. On two or three occasions we were in the front stalls. It was a world of enchantment, an extravaganza of gold, bright chandeliers and crimson comfort. This was even before the curtain had gone up on the magic of the stage! I truly believe that we were treated kindly, smiled at and spoken to as if it was quite the usual thing to find a couple of urchins sitting in the best seats. The gallery was quite different. We were shoved around and on the wall was a warning a foot high "Beware of pickpockets". There must be a moral there somewhere.

If the show was a sell out we didn't do so badly either. Small folding chairs were hired out to those queuing for tickets and we hired ourselves out to sit on the chairs. It was sixpence well spent by the patrons, especially in rotten weather, for it saved them a wait of an hour or more. We in turn were entertained by the buskers who played the clown, sang, danced, did handstands and cartwheels. War medals were prominently displayed. There was often a one-man band, complete with drums, mouth-organ, washboard, concertina and cymbals.

Drury Lane Theatre was popular with everyone, audiences, actors, staff, buskers, kids, everyone. The front entrance in Catherine Street was impressive and I hope it still is, but it was the large revolving stage and the exceptionally good access for props via Drury Lane that enabled the management to put on truly spectacular shows. There were never any free tickets for these.

The Garden of Allah for example was sold out from its opening in June 1920 until the theatre closed for rebuilding in April 1921. I never saw the show, but the prologue was an entertainment in itself.

From the bottom of Endell Street, where they were stabled, six or eight camels were led, pushed and prodded by a small army of keepers dressed in white flowing robes, along Bow Street via Russell Street into Drury Lane. The camels shuffled contemptuously along, showing their great yellow teeth and occasionally spitting horribly. They were accompanied all the way by an even bigger army of excited shouting kids. I used to be at the front until I got spat on. After that I was content to be a less conspicuous target.

At the theatre the beasts went up a ramp and through the large doors which were promptly shut in our faces. Even outside Drury Lane we could hear the enthusiastic applause. The big scene, according to Mrs Hutchings, one of the dressers, was a raging sandstorm for which wind machines would blow peaflour across the stage. This scene was less than popular with the stage hands who had to clear up afterwards.

Apparently the camels were not all that keen either and caused a certain amount of apprehension about what they might or might not do. Their departure about the time of the first interval was a relief backstage. We would be waiting of course for the doors to open, the ramp to come down and the trek back to Endell Street. After a few evenings of this I went back to the front of the theatre. People were more entertaining than camels and more profitable.

There was genuine distress when the theatre closed for rebuilding. The carpenters and some of the stage hands were kept on, but the usherettes and the dressers had a lean time for about a year.

Mrs Hutchings went to work for Robinsons, a swank woman's outfitters in the Strand, but returned to old Drury as soon as it reopened. She was another small, thin, energetic woman always on the run and very much the boss of the family.

Mr Hutchings, fat, jovial, worked in the market as a porter, liked his pint, but took good care not to get drunk. They had two young daughters who they adored and watched over with great care. Mrs Hutchings was sure that one day they would shine as stars at the old Drury. They would have been great as the ugly sisters in Cinderella.

We unkindly called them the ugly ducklings, but they became more personable as they grew older, not swans perhaps, but friendly well turned-out ducks. I envied them. They had a proper family life and Mrs Hutchings was a teetotaller. She and Mother got on well together despite, or perhaps because of, their knife-sharp differences of opinion. With Mother no-one needed to cross a gypsy's palm with silver to have their fortune told — with Mother you got it for free, friend or foe. And Mrs Hutchings was a worthy antagonist, adding to

Mother's respect and enjoyment of her company. She was also generous, worse luck.

Take the boots for example. Very smart on the stage, I'm sure, beautifully made of soft black kid, shaped to fit the calf, buttoned up the sides, pointed toes and bloody great high heels. And the rotten things fitted me! As it was winter and I was down to my last pair of plimsolls, Mother called me an ungrateful whining brat when I perched before her like a tear-stained stork and begged her not to make me wear them for school. Her only concession was to have the heels sawn off by the carpenter who also worked at the theatre. This tilted me backwards instead of forwards. To correct this I walked with my shoulders forward but my bum stuck out, no longer a stork, more like a constipated chicken. These boots didn't last long. I jumped into puddles, scraped along the gutters, even into Cobbler's pee. Mr Jones was scandalized, but helped me, while I sat in his van in my socks, by dropping fourteen pound weights on the toes. Mrs Hutchings was sorrowful and Mother was furious when they had had to concede that the boots were done for. Victory and chilblains were mine for the rest of the winter.

Some of the dresses, with alterations, were not too outrageous, but one caused me agonies of embarrassment. It was a lovely dress, obviously expensive, in pure white lace and a wide blue silk sash, and it came down to my ankles. I only wore it for church, but once again I did not fit in but stood out from the righteous in their sober Sunday clothes. Mother would command me to stand up straight and I prayed to the Lord to make me invisible. I took no notice of Mother and the Lord took no notice of me. The final irony was that on one Sunday morning I made Mother so angry that she ripped the dress in half. I put it together again. I did this when Mother was not around and it was not to go to church in. I wanted the dress so that I could play the leading part in our own, our very own theatre called "The Grotto".

We used to rig up a stage in a corner behind the buildings, divide it off with old curtains and decorate it with a few fancy stones and flowers. We made up our own plays mainly on the theme *Poor Girl and the Prince*. We charged a ha'penny to anyone daft enough to come and watch, and made them queue up as well while we did a little busking until the show was ready.

It was great fun, especially when we recruited a few more boys to help us with our version of *Richard III* which was somewhat shorter than Shakespeare's. The one part we were all certain about was that Richard should cry out "A horse, a horse, my kingdom for a horse" and then die. The problem arose when Richard refused to die and started to knock hell out of Richmond's army, all three of them. Somehow the audience got involved and real blood began to flow. Finally there was an almighty row between some of the parents. The committee, consisting of Maud and myself, decided to suspend performances for the summer and went to play in the Sands of Dee instead.

The Sands of Dee was not far from Bush House. It was a large piece of land that lay derelict for years and had become overgrown with weeds, grass and wild flowers like Ragged Robin. Why we called it the Sands of Dee I don't know, but we had hours of pleasure there, making up stories about adventures in far away places. I had a bit of an edge over Maud in this because there was one place I kept for myself only.

Quite by chance during one of my wanderings it started to rain heavily, and I went inside the doorway to Australia House. I became interested in the photographs and the doorman asked if I would like to see a film about Australia. It was free, on my life. It was also very comfortable. I sat through the same film about four times. When I came out I was given a large juicy apple and the rain had stopped. After that, whenever I was alone and feeling down, I used to nip into Australia House for some second-hand sunshine, a geography lesson, a free apple and a chat with the doorman. According to him thousands of people, particularly ex-servicemen unable to find work in England, were emigrating on what was called "assisted passage". But I kept all this to myself as I wanted no one to spoil it. I didn't trust even Maud not to tell the others who would have trooped in en masse.

Crossing over the Strand from Australia House is Norfolk Street which runs steeply down to the Embankment. We used to dare each other to go down the hill on a pair of decrepit old skates. There were large offices either side of the road and when these closed there were few pedestrians about. It was my bad luck to catch the elbow of one of those who, for a gentleman so well dressed, used the most frightful language and called a policeman. The policeman informed Mother who told him the quickest way to Bow Street. I expected the hiding of a lifetime. Instead the gentleman was called a silly old fool and I escaped with a half-hearted clip on the ear — and she was cold sober at the time!

Although I was pleased by the way Mother dismissed the matter, I was apprehensive that the policeman might take a different view. For we were not unknown at Bow Street. We had been summoned to appear there only a month or so before.

It all began one Saturday morning when I was scrubbing our section of the stone stairs of the tenements. A zinc bucket, really hot water and lots of effort were needed to get them really clean. I had almost finished when a lolloping great hulk of a porter, Mr Long, walked over my work with his dirty great feet. I asked him what the hell he was playing at and was he too drunk to see where he was going. He threatened me with a good hiding. I called Mother who had just returned from the pawn shop with our Sunday clothes. She described Mr Long's parentage in explicit detail and, furthermore, offered to stick a hat-pin up his nose — or some other part of his anatomy.

Mr Long stormed off to Bow Street and we were duly summoned to appear. Although we had two witnesses on our side and Mother was supremely confident, I was not so sure. On the appointed day a small crowd of us went off to Bow Street Station ready for the battle.

We were about to march in when Mr Long came out to announce he had dropped the charge and that everyone was invited for a drink at *The Falstaff*. He gave me two shillings and an apron full of cherries that he had cadged from one of his mates at the market.

It was a fine day, the sun shone. Mother and Mr Long proposed each other's health, peace and harmony prevailed, all wrongs were forgiven and forgotten. And so it was with the skates. No more was said, but I stayed away from Norfolk Street for some time.

I was not then aware of a common factor between Mr Long's unexpected and uncharacteristic change of mind and the lack of any action concerning the skates and Mother's high-handed dismissal of the policeman. Quite unknown to me I had a part-time guardian angel. I realize now, trying to write all this out of my system, trying to rid myself of the bitter cud of hatred towards my mother and brother, that I had more than one such angel, the Pennington Bickfords for example, and my headmaster, Mr Gerrard. Such is the change of perspective that old age brings.

This particular guardian angel walked around with marbles in the fingers of one glove and administered instant justice with an extremely painful clip around the head of any petty transgressor he caught on his patch. Many kids and their parents had reason to be grateful to him for keeping them out of court. He it was who had a quiet word with Mr Long and also with the young constable whose dignity had been upset by Mother.

My angel was a Mr Tubbs, a policeman at Bow Street Station, who lived with his wife and young son in another block of the buildings. Although respected, the family did not mix with the neighbours. This was understandable, but hard on the son who had a lonely life but who later had the rare distinction of winning a scholarship for further education. I certainly would not claim him for a friend, but I did introduce him to Mr Jones and the infamous Cobbler, and was in turn introduced to the infamous Richard the Third and his cry "A horse, a horse, my kingdom for a horse". On such a slender acquaintanceship, I was invited to his birthday parties.

The first one was a revelation to me. The flat was comfortably furnished and had a whole shelf of books. The birthday tea was wonderful with all sorts of sandwiches and biscuits, an iced cake with red candles, and, I still love it, mandarins in jelly with lashings of ice cream.

Mrs Tubbs was friendly enough but remote. She was very, very respectable. Mr Tubbs was present at the first party and I liked him very much. But the next time I met him was one Saturday night when escorting Mother home. He helped us up the stairs with the light from his torch. I was bitterly ashamed but, if anything, his attitude was kinder than before.

I found out years later from Mrs Hutchings that he was concerned for my welfare. His concern helped me out of the scrape with Mr Long and the gentleman in Norfolk Street, but it did me very great harm later on. I shall come to that in due course.

As I have said already, Saturday morning was the time to redeem our clothes for wear on Sunday. Then with the remainder of her week's wages in her pocket,

Mother would be off to *The Falstaff* and she would stay there until it was time to leave for the Exchequer and Audit Department on Blackfriars Embankment. I would go with her for she was truly drunk by then and needed a guiding hand. Her job was to clean the wide stone stairs with hearthstone. This was really hard work but when she was done, the stairs were immaculate and she would be sober.

Then we were off up New Bridge Street into Farringdon Street, with a stop at the *King Lud* for a quick pint for Mother and for me a "Buster", a large roll filled with meat. Neither of us had had any dinner and I was famished. Then it was over Holborn Viaduct and into Smithfield Market just at closing time. With me in tow Mother would push her way to the front of the crowd bidding for surplus meat being auctioned off cheaply. At times you could get enough meat to last a whole week for only a few shillings, but, once again, without refrigeration, this would be money wasted in the summer. On a hot evening pork sausages were sometimes literally given away.

I would take the meat home and put it in the coolest place, a box on top of the coal cupboard. Mother went straight back to *The Falstaff* until I was able to cajole her away, hopefully before eleven p.m.

It was this Saturday ritual, with its sordid drunken ending that finally convinced Mr Tubbs to have a word with Mother about my welfare.

CHAPTER
TWO

From Orphans to Debutantes

It was summer and I was coming up to my eleventh birthday. The atmosphere in the tenements was oppressive. As Mother became increasingly trapped by drink and debt her temper grew even more unpredictable. My quarrels with Bill, my brother, became more violent as he seemed to have neither the wit nor the will to understand the mess we were in. I had seen the effect of such court cases on other families — and they had fathers!

What I had not foreseen was that those so concerned with my welfare, including Mr Tubbs, had consulted with and had been persuaded by my mother that I would be better off in an orphanage. It broke my heart then and it breaks my heart now to know that she did the persuading. Mother love indeed! Even animals would fight to the death to defend their young, but not my mother, not for me.

I was told quite casually what was to happen, on a Sunday while peeling potatoes for dinner; the only full dinner with meat and vegetables that we had had that week. I was a girl . . . getting older and needing more looking after . . . that's all . . . I was not to ask any questions. The next day, instead of taking our clothes to the pawn shop, she took me to the orphanage in Stockwell.

As we entered through the high, elegant wrought iron gates I allowed myself to hope. Leading off from either side of the tree-lined drive were rows of red brick villas that in the sunlight looked not unattractive. We were led straight to one of these villas to be interviewed by the matron or house mother in her sitting room-cum-office. She was short, plump, white haired and wore a simple high necked long black dress. She was quite charming. The doctor was summoned and, after a brief examination of my throat and chest, pronounced me fit.

It was arranged that I would be accepted at the start of the next school term and everything, food, accommodation, clothing, education, would be provided by the orphanage.

I thought I was in luck. I chattered away like a half-witted chimpanzee to all my school friends, to Mrs Bickford, Mr Gerrard, Mr Tubbs, Mr Jones, to anyone who would listen, even to Cobbler. This was to be the start of a grand new adventure. Oh God, what a difference between theory and practice, between appearance and reality. Mother took me on the tram and I was already beginning to feel vaguely apprehensive.

My parting that morning with Mr Jones had been awkward and constrained.

"Don't forget now, Ethel girl. Me and old Cobbler will be around here somewhere if you need us. Don't forget to write." He pressed a two shilling piece into my hand and went off swearing at one of the porters.

The house mother's greeting was brisk and she left us alone in the dining room to say our goodbyes. But Mother walked away without a word. I stood at the window in that empty barn of a room and watched her go away from me. That familiar indomitable stride did not falter. She did not turn even to wave. I felt utterly alone, utterly wretched. I wanted to run after her, to throw my arms about her, to beg forgiveness. Forgiveness for what? . . . for being born?

I waited an hour alone until the other girls came clattering in from school. They immediately began to set up long trestle tables and chairs which had been stacked against one wall. The house mother and her assistant appeared and I was introduced. The girls stood quiet, passive, uninterested, uninvolved. We stood in our places at the table in order of age while grace was said. From a scullery at the end of the room, plates of bread and butter and chipped mugs of tea were passed along. That was it, that was tea. The eldest girl got the most, the youngest the least. There was nothing more to eat or drink until breakfast next morning. No wonder the girls were apathetic; they were half starved.

After tea there was the washing up to be done, tables and chairs to be stacked away and counterpanes in the dormitory upstairs to be folded. Then we were "free" until seven thirty when we prepared for bed. We were watched at all times.

There were thirty girls to each villa and I made friends with not one of them. I cannot remember their names, or even what they looked like. I was traumatized almost from the start. I was used to hard work, scrubbing and polishing floors, but this was hard labour. I was used to going hungry, but not all the time. I was used to punishment, but this was different. No blows were struck; no blows were needed. In the name of Christian charity, a petty inflexible tyranny ruled by enforced silence, solitary confinement and public humiliation.

We had no private possessions. Our clothes were not our own, nothing was personalized. It was a matter of chance how well each change of clothes fitted. Once a week we were dressed in "special clothes", good quality clothes, outdoor clothes, but it was the same hit and miss affair. If they touched, they fitted, and that included the boots. The dresses were navy blue alpaca with red trimmings, with a raincoat to match in winter.

In these we were lined up in twos, marched over Lambeth Bridge to Westminster Abbey, rested in Victoria Tower Gardens and then marched back again. Perhaps we talked and laughed. I don't remember. I was in a daze most of the time, wondering whether I dare jump on a tram without money. I knew that it was no good going home, but perhaps Mr Jones would take me to Lambeth in his van.

I couldn't write to him for we were allowed to write only one letter a week to a parent or guardian. The letter was censored and at any word of complaint it was torn up and another dictated. You were then sent to the dormitory with its rows of iron beds, straw palliases and ice cold sheets. In summer it was cool, in winter it was freezing.

Each morning we were woken at six a.m. by the house mother and we stripped our beds for her inspection. I had become accustomed to the ritual of punishment. For complaining about the meagre meals, porridge for breakfast, half cold stew for dinner, two slices of bread for tea, I was made to eat alone in the scullery for three days. For some equally trivial offences I had to scrub tables in the backyard. The water was cold, the wind colder. My fingers were covered with broken chilblains and every stroke of the brush was agony to me. I nearly fainted when I was finally called in.

Worse was to follow. The combination of cold, misery and malnutrition resulted in my wetting the bed for the first time in my life. I was horrified but the house mother was almost triumphant as she called each girl to inspect the bed. For punishment I went without breakfast and was made to polish the whole dormitory floor before I went to school.

Every night I would pray that it would not happen again. I tried to force myself to stay awake, but it was no use. Next morning it was the same degrading ritual but now after they had been inspected by everyone, I had to gather up my bedclothes and take them to the laundry.

The laundry was in the grounds and I had to explain my conduct to the person in charge. I had to speak up so that everyone could hear. I was made to stand on a block of wood in front of a large bath and had to wash out the clothes myself. No-one else spoke to me, I was totally ignored. This went on morning after morning, the cold disdain, the isolation, the shame of being unclean.

Mother came to visit me once a month and I would weep and ask why I should be so punished. Her face would set like a rock and she would say nothing. One month she brought me a beautifully dressed doll, a present from Mrs Bickford. I threw it into the communal cupboard and never touched it again.

I was rescued from my misery by an outbreak of scarlet fever. I was one of the first victims and was sent to the infirmary to be in isolation in a small room tiled from floor to ceiling, with a small window overlooking the Stockwell Road. Only a nurse visited me to see that I was washed and to bring me a meal which I often threw down the toilet. At last a doctor came. He was very gentle and talked to me for a long time. Between sobs I told him about the tenements, St Clement Danes, the Market, Cobbler. He walked about the room, asked questions. Finally he said he was sending me home. At first I could not believe it. I was immediately taken to a better room and even the meals improved.

As soon as I was fit enough, Mother came to collect me. She was just as dour, just as grim, only slightly mollified by the gift of a whole outfit of clothing, including an awful alpaca dress. My dance of joy was cut short by a cuff on the ear, but I didn't care. I was going home.

Yet that year in the orphanage had changed me. I was scarred for life, but unlike the scars left by shrapnel and cancer, these scars do now show on the outside. Although I have received many great acts of kindness, a great deal of love and compassion, there remains within that mistrust, that fear of betrayal, of being alone in some awful place from which there is no escape. Falling bombs and flaming trees haunt my dreams, but it is the terror of being alone that wakes me sobbing in the night.

Others also had changed during that year. Mother was thinner, harder, drinking less, constrained by a court order to repay her debts. Bill was taciturn and lived in a fantasy world of his own, which I did not enter. Maud was no longer my best friend and I no longer had a deciding voice in the gang which itself had changed.

Cobbler seemed pleased. He seized the front of my hated alpaca dress, rocked me to and fro, then wiped his dirty great muzzle all over me. I pulled his ears, rubbed my knuckles round and round the white star in the middle of his forehead, told him that he was a villain, a horror and I loved him very much. Mr Jones was not so cordial, upset because I had not written. I explained that I couldn't, that I had nearly run away to find him. His reserve vanished and we were friends again. But even this reunion was marred.

Trade was slack, everyone wanted credit which he could not afford; he and his wife were homesick for Wales. Something inside me died a little and I began to see less of him as a defence against the pain of parting.

Mrs Bickford made a great fuss of me but I tried to avoid her by going to St Paul's Church. The vicar, Mr Hart Davies, was a tall old man with white hair, his wife short, stout, extremely well spoken, but reserved. They were both kindly, well intentioned, but lacked the warmth of the Bickfords. They had a fat, ugly Pekinese, blind in one eye and, according to their maid, spoilt rotten with special meals and a satin cushion to sleep on.

St Paul's Church, despite its garden and connections with writers and actors, is a dull old church and I soon returned to St Clement Danes.

One evening after service Mrs Bickford invited me back to the vicarage at the top of St Clements Inn. I was still wearing the orphanage clothes which I insisted on calling my prison uniform. Mother was furious but I had grown a little harder too and taunted her to strike me, "Hit me, go on, hit me! I'll wear the rotten things and I'll tell everyone why. I've been to prison! I've a good mind to paint arrows all over them, knickers and all!"

Mrs Bickford sat me down in an enormous shabby Berkeley chair and we talked and talked and talked. Within a week I had a complete change of clothes and, with a large party of other children, I was on a train to Shoreham in Sussex where the Bickfords had a very large house. I had accepted the invitation of a holiday with caution and did not share in the general excitement as we boarded the train. I managed to get a window seat and sat with my cardboard suitcase clutched tightly in front of me.

My mistrust began to thaw as I watched the slowly changing soft green and yellow countryside. There were glimpses of streams and hedges flecked with flowers. All the cows seemed to be brown or brown and white, not Cobbler's chestnut, nor roan, nor bay, nor sorrel, but toffee-coloured. And the sheep! I was more excited about the sheep than I had been about the camels in Drury Lane!

As soon as we arrived at the house we had a whacking great meal. I had never eaten maize before, nor since, even as corn on the cob, but at that time I thought maize pudding a great treat.

The house was spacious with separate apartments for the Pennington Bickfords, a huge dining room, and two dormitories, one for the boys and one for the girls. The gardens at the front of the house were a riot of colour with roses, hydrangeas, foxgloves, snapdragons, lupins, all sorts of flowers I had never seen before. At the back was an orchard, a vegetable garden and a large barn where we were allowed to play if it rained. It didn't rain, I'm sure of it. One golden day following another, each day a different expedition deep into the countryside, or by the sea.

But I must not forget Mr Dukes, the gardener. He was old, bent like a tree and, despite the heat, never took off his heavy coat or battered hat. His speech was soft, slow and gentle, but those crooked limbs and gnarled hands could move fast when need be. I was chasing after a ball when in one continuous movement Mr Dukes straightened up, pulled me to a stop, stepped in front, bent down, picked up a snake by its tail and cracked it like a whip. As he held it out to me, the forked tongue slid back between the jaws and I screamed.

Mr Pennington Bickford and the other children came running. There were lots of oohs and ahs. Mr Dukes was congratulated and we were all treated to an impromptu lesson on snakes. Our one was a male adder and normally Mr Dukes would not have killed it but I might have been bitten and the bite would have been poisonous and so on and so on. Reluctant to relinquish my role as heroine, I overcame my repugnance and accepted the snake as a souvenir. I sold it to Jimmy Connally for sixpence.

Immediately facing the house and overhung with trees was a narrow lane deep in shadow from side to side, with just a dapple of sunlight. It had a strange hypnotic effect upon us, not frightening, but we walked along it quietly as if we were in a church or cathedral. The lane led down to the railway line and over the line down to the village which was dominated by the busy mill with wagons delivering wheat and others taking away flour. At times the shops and houses had a faint dusting of flour, which gave them a quaint fairy-tale quality. I was entranced, to me it would have looked perfect on the stage at Drury Lane. We went through the village and crossed over a creek by rowing boat to get to the beach.

Mr Pennington Bickford had an old open topped car called Gertrude into which he would pack as many children as possible. Every time we came to a bend the springs would groan and we all had to lean in the opposite direction. When we came to a slope Gertrude gave up altogether and we had to pile out and push. We spent more time pushing than riding, but it was great fun.

We expected to visit churches, but we also went to various farms, to a boat-house with the smell of newly planed wood, paint and tar.

What impressed me most was the sense of space, the sea and the sky melting away into the distance and the quiet that was never really quiet, the cry of birds, the noises of cows and sheep, the farm labourers with their horses and tackle, echoing and re-echoing church bells. At night I could hear the small animals in the eaves and the hoot of owls; at morning the call of cockerels and dogs barking.

It was a good time, my belly was full and I laughed easily, but by the end of the second week I longed for the sight of a London bus and my mother.

I make no attempt to excuse or explain. I can't, that's just the way it was.

Mother's welcome on my return from holiday was typically taciturn and included a telling off for wasting money on sending her a postcard, but nevertheless I felt more at ease in my old surroundings.

I made friends with a large easy going family who had recently moved into the tenements. The Hardys were an attractive well-spoken couple from Edinburgh, with five young children.

Mr Hardy had trained as a musician in a Scottish regiment and came unscathed through the war except for a minor shoulder wound. He was both a cornet player and a drummer and did well with various bands and orchestras working the clubs and dance halls. He had a wide range of cornets, trumpets, drums, cymbals, and triangles which hung from hooks on the walls.

All these instruments and five children left little room for furniture, but there was always a barrel of apples and a box of oranges for the children to dip into at any time. Mrs Hardy was quiet, serenely indifferent to anything and anybody other than her children.

I got into a habit of taking the two youngest for walks, Alice aged six months in a smart bassinet and Sarah aged two years trotting alongside. In Long Acre Sarah became particularly interested in a theatrical costumiers who sold everything from make up to armour. The staff made a great fuss of Alice who was a lovely baby. All went well until Sarah knocked over several pieces of armour with what is known as the domino effect. Armour, dresses, wigs, hats, all sorts cascaded down in a spectacular fashion. Alice began to bawl, Sarah prostrate beneath several breast plates did the same. One of the staff, a Frenchman with an elaborately curled moustached, jumped up and down in an ecstasy of rage. We retreated in a hurry and were not made welcome again.

I described the Hardys as easy going, but easy come, easy go is perhaps more accurate. Despite their lack of possessions they seemed to spend freely. There were always a few coppers for broken biscuits, complete with mice droppings, or cornets from Jacks where the ice cream was made in the back parlour and served from a large metal container packed round with crushed ice.

More than most Mrs Hardy would order their dinner of roast beef and baked potatoes to be cooked by the local baker whose bread was sold by weight, hot and aromatic across the counter. In those days some shops used to stay open almost as late as the pubs. Drury Lane with the flaring naphtha lamps was a lively savoury place and my belly would flap against my backbone as I went for jellied eels and mash, or faggots and pease pudding, or half a sheep's head already cooked and full of juices. But both of the Hardys were generous and I often ended up with a bite of supper.

Mother was darkly suspicious of the Hardys. They had butter, we had margarine; they had real milk, we had condensed milk out of a tin; they had whole herrings, we were sometimes down to half a one; they had real strawberry or raspberry jam, we had an anonymous sticky mixture sold by the pennyworth alongside the paraffin and firewood at the general store. The children had new shoes. A smartly turned out Mr Hardy went by taxi with his drums and sometimes gave me sixpence to help him carry them down the stairs. No good could come of such profligacy.

Mother was proved right when the Hardys did a moonlight flit owing several weeks' rent and other debts. How they got away with all that gear and those children in the middle of the night without detection we never knew.

"Practice makes perfect," said Mother and was so pleased that the very next day she took us to Highgate Cemetery to visit father's grave.

We enjoyed playing among the tombstones and one large black marble slab dedicated to some dear departed made an excellent table on which to enjoy our bloater paste sandwiches and our drink made from lemonade powder. Nearby was Waterlow Park with grass thick with buttercups, almost like being in the country.

On the tram home I was often, nearly always, heartily sick and had to stand with my head over the side near the driver who was less than enthusiastic. If he dared complain, Mother would be ready with a diatribe against the tram company, the state of the tram and the incompetence of the driver.

It was a similar story when on Bank Holidays we went to Hampstead Heath, except that we walked miles and miles. We never had money to spend, we enjoyed the fun of the fair for nothing, laughing at the antics of others. On the way home I would be sick, someone was sure to make an adverse comment and Wham! Bang! They were glad to get off at the next stop. The poor driver had no such luck. The Lord loveth a joyful heart, so Mother was all right. Nothing made her more joyful than a good row after a day out.

One of the days to Hampstead Heath that started full of promise but ended dismally for me was in the company of Miss Olivia Burleigh, an actress who often appeared on the stage at the Strand Theatre. She lived in a luxurious flat close by Bow Street police station. Mother went there at least three times a week to clean and polish and I sometimes went with her. I had to take my shoes off before walking on the thick richly patterned carpet that had to be damped down with used tea leaves before it was swept with hand brush and pan. The dining room was very fine, the top of the sideboard reflecting candle sticks and bowls of fruit. Beside the grapes was a small pair of scissors with enamelled handles and fine scrolled blades. It was not until Miss Burleigh delicately offered me a grape, snipping just one from a large bunch, that I associated scissors with grapes. I didn't know what to do with the pips, so I swallowed them. Miss Burleigh seemed mildly surprised but continued to make a fuss of me whenever I went to the flat. I used to dream of being like her, cool, elegant, posh and knowing what to do with grape pips.

Then came the offer of a bus ride and lunch at the *Spaniards Inn* at Hampstead. Would I care to go? Would I care — I was so excited I couldn't sleep the night before. From the bedroom window I watched the bobbies on the beat, one of them having a crafty fag; watched the cleaners hose down the street and the sun top the buildings as the first traders arrived at the market. Mother inspected my head for nits, my ears and my finger nails for dirt and, with the usual dire words of warning, stomped off to work.

At ten a.m. in my best clothes from Uncle's, I dashed along to Bow Street. The day was just right for sitting upstairs on an open-topped bus and there was I, Ethel Parker, companion to an actress who had trodden the boards with Ivor Novello!

The Spaniards Inn was a fairly modest building transformed by flowers, flowers everywhere, in tubs, in hanging baskets and on the tables. Miss Burleigh was expected and there were smiles and a couple of "hello, darlings" as we were ushered to our table. After much discussion with the waiter she settled down to her meal. A bottle of white wine, some melon, a lemon sole with a veritable harvest of vegetables, followed by fruit salad and cream, followed by coffee and a liqueur. I waited and watched and waited. All round me food was disappearing at an alarming rate. At last, with a flourish like a conjuror producing a rabbit out of a hat, a waiter presented me with a small slice of cake. I let it lie on my plate and sat silent. Miss Burleigh, radiant and contented, asked me quite gaily "Not hungry, dear?" and wolfed down my piece of cake.

I was not sick on the silent journey home, though I fervently hoped Miss Burleigh would be. Back at Bow Street I offered a polite "thank you" and made straight for St Clement Danes where I prayed that Miss Olivia Burleigh, an actress, would have the most God awful bellyache.

There was just the lift of an eyebrow and a hint of a smile on Mother's face when I refused to go to the flat again. No questions were asked, no recriminations made. Instead, she said that as she had an hour free she was going along to the House "to see what that bugger Churchill is up to. You come too."

Some of my happiest moments were spent in the Strangers' Gallery. I cannot recall a word of what was said, but I remember the taste of the pennyworth of humbugs and those rare precious shared moments of companionship with Mother. To her the Commons was better than the theatre, it cost nothing for a start and she sat there like a battered Queen Victoria refusing to be amused. She detested Churchill, distrusted Lloyd George, but approved of Baldwin. I am embarrassed that I sat there in blissful ignorance while the fate of millions may have been debated, for Westminster was still the heart of an Empire.

I still remain totally unimpressed by the worn out rhetoric and recycled promises of politicians, but I'm a sucker for the pomp and pageantry of power. The sound of a military band still sets my tired old feet tapping and I remember with nostalgia the days when I used to race down the Mall for even a glimpse of the Trooping the Colour.

For two or three years I had tried to see something of the Trooping the Colour and each time I had been disappointed. I was too small to keep my place in the crowd. In 1921, however, I went with Ginger Tom and Ivy and no-one was daft enough to shove Tom around. As the first troops went past he lifted me up so that I stood on his massive shoulders and had a splendid view of the cavalry and their magnificent horses, but I was unprepared for the impact that Queen Mary made on me.

Mother was a true blue Tory down to her toe nails and would not tolerate criticism of the monarchy as such, although she had few illusions about royalty as individuals. They used toilet paper as did the rest of us (she didn't put it quite like that, and we used cut up newspaper anyway).

61

Queen Mary in a carriage came along in advance of the King by some minutes and she *was* different — regal, majestic, expecting and receiving homage. As she turned her unsmiling face in my direction, the force of her personality, the strength of her character overwhelmed me. It was a physical shock and all over in a moment, but if she had beckoned I would have followed her anywhere without question.

King George, bearded, upright, riding alone on his horse ahead of more troops, was kingly enough, but to me he was just Queen Mary's husband. I could not have explained it then and it all seems a bit daft when I try to write it down now. You can make of it what you will and if you don't like it you can lump it, but I took it for granted that twenty-three years later she should speak directly to me out of an office of some thirty or more other clerks.

It took even the management by surprise, though that was her style, but I answered her questions calmly and without hesitation. Princess Margaret, hovering about in the background, did not seem pleased and the chief clerk was full of shocked indignation.

"You should have curtsied!" How do you do that while sitting down? "You were showing too much leg!" He had never made that objection before, the obnoxious little squit. And so it went on, but I was oblivious to criticism, a dream had been realized.

To return to 1921, after the ceremony Tom and Ivy gave me a smashing dinner of bangers and mash, then took me on to Regent's Park and my first visit to the Zoo. My mind was so crowded with other images that I cannot remember much, except that some of the animals seemed rather sad, but I always feel that about the Zoo.

We rarely went to Regent's Park, preferring to spend fine days during the holidays in St James's Park with its huge beds of brilliant red geraniums, the lovely lake with all sorts of wild fowl and the impeccably dressed ladies and gentlemen promenading beneath the trees.

From there, just across Constitution Hill, we went into Green Park, not so attractive, but popular with families playing football and cricket. Then on to Hyde Park and Rotten Row. I felt downright jealous of those girls on their ponies, with all the right gear, especially those in family groups, and tried to make the other kids laugh by bobbing up and down with one hand holding my bum and my eyes and nose turned up in exquisite scorn.

At the Serpentine there was always a hope of seeing some straw-hatted would-be gent desperately going round in small circles. I wonder how many romances died the death on that lake? It must have been difficult to play the gallant while sweating profusely and the sardonic boatman at the landing stage asking your girlfriend with mock solicitude, "Did you get a bit wet, Miss?" Especially so when watched by a group of grinning kids.

And there was always someone to make fun of at Speakers' Corner. I was fool enough to stand in front of a small group baiting an earnest young man in full flood about communism. I called him Commissar Comic Cuts (a quote from my mother about a trade union leader) and the young man made a sudden grab for my arm. I turned and fled but he soon caught me and fiercely demanded, "Do you know what would have happened if I had been a Cossack and you a Russian peasant?"

I shook my head and replied tremulously, "I think I'm going to pee!" — and I did.

The young man roared with laughter and returned to his soap box in high good humour. Discomforted and uncomfortable, I made my way back home to wash out my knickers before Mother got back.

When you consider that London was one of the major cities of the world, the major city so we were told, rich in wealth, history and spectacle, it was disgracefully deficient in public lavatories. Cabbies and carters were allowed by law to urinate against the offside wheel of their vehicles and did so with a casual disregard to passers-by, but I had to be near bursting before I did a Windy Winnie down some hopefully deserted street.

Could it be the unnatural retention of pee causing guardsmen to sometimes faint and fall to the ground? With the coming of Spring, the swallow and the social Season, how did the debutantes manage? Did they have chamber pots in those limousines queuing up bumper to bumper down Pall Mall waiting to get into Buckingham Palace Yard? I never saw any of the bejewelled daughters of the aristocracy nip out for a crafty pee behind a tree.

Mixing with the crowds gathered to look at and comment upon the finery and the feathers, Maud and I used to pull faces at the beauties and their haughty elderly escorts and chant:

"Where ere I go, I take my po and a little bit of tissue paper."

Childish stuff, but we were children.

The start of the Season brought tourists from all over the world, particularly from America. They had only to ask for directions to the next street and we appointed ourselves as their guides. Americans are sometimes presented as gullible culture vultures, but we found them shrewd, questioning and careful with their money, knowing more than we about the history of the places they wanted to see. We knew exactly where the places were and the best way of getting there. I think that we gave them value. We made them laugh a lot. They obviously thought that we were quaint, possibly out of Dickens.

With Dickens I was on a winner. I had never read one of his books but he was my trump card, my ace in the hole. Mother had actually lived and worked in the Old Curiosity Shop when she was thirteen years old. She was a maid of all work and only stayed a few weeks, but live and work there she did until my grandfather discovered she had developed a taste for port wine, taking crafty sips on the sly, though apparently with the knowledge of her employers. In a fit of moral outrage grandfather made her leave. It was ironic that within a few years he drank away the profits of three hansom cabs which had to be sold to settle his debts.

He was in his time literally a terror on wheels, always ready for a wager, a fight or a drink, and once won a bet by driving up the marble staircase of one of those large old houses near Clare Street. The horse, my grandfather and the staircase survived, but the cab was a wreck. Often he drove himself and his horses day and night until he fell into a drunken sleep with the reins still in his hands. The horse would find its own way home to where grandmother would be waiting. She would unharness the horse, go through grandfather's pockets hoping to find enough for the rent and the next day's meal and then bundle him, wet or dry, into the stable to sleep it off with the horse.

Grandfather would be up in a few hours, take a fresh horse and another cab and start all over again. Grandmother would feed and groom yesterday's horse and clean up the cab. It was a wretched life with a wretched end. She died miserably of a stroke in a run down infirmary in the City Road. Grandfather lived to ninety years of age. I was then seven and remember him as tall, erect, dignified, with a splendid mane of white hair and a fine moustache. I used to sit on his knee and listen to the tales of some of his more well-known passengers. Dickens, for example, Thackeray, the Duchess of — who was often more drunk than he was and, though her skinny fingers were loaded with diamonds, never gave a tip.

He had once driven a coach and pair in the Lord Mayor's Show. If only I could remember it all. When he fell ill with pneumonia, Mother nursed him right to the end, changing and washing his nightgown and bed linen without complaint. At the same time she kept working at most of her other jobs and somehow kept Bill and me fed.

When grandfather died, well respected and stony broke, the vicar gave a moving sermon full of praise; several old ladies in the congregation wept copiously. Mother sat stony faced and dry eyed and when the service was over, hurried off to her next job.

Grandfather died in late October and so missed his favourite pageant always held on the ninth of November, the Lord Mayor's Show. That year it was a great military parade. It was the year of the Armistice, 1918 and I remember nothing about it. According to Mother, rejoicing went on for days and nights and all I can recall is getting lost among the seething crowds in Trafalgar Square, an event hardly sufficient to blot out all other memory of the time.

Up till then my mother had been strong, formidable, indomitable. Perhaps the nightmare of coping for the first time with her awful drunken stupor, coming so soon after grandfather's death, was the trauma that made me forget everything else.

I certainly remember other Lord Mayor's Shows. They were for Londoners the best, the proudest pageants of them all with horse-drawn carriages for the Livery Companies, the magnificent Lord Mayor's coach itself with his Lord Nibs clothed in scarlet. There were pikemen, musketeers, military bands, dozens and dozens of wonderfully decorated floats usually reflecting some aspect of London life. And what is more, we were given a day off from school to watch it. We used to stand opposite the Inner Temple gardens on the Victoria Embankment. When the procession had passed we belted through the side streets to Temple Bar to watch His Nibs arrive for the ceremony at the Courts of Justice.

Mr Gerrard our headmaster retold each year the history of the election of the Lord Mayor of London and each year I must have dozed off. I am no scholar and I still find it impossible to remember who bashed who, when and where in these interminable conflicts between the Crown and the Church and the City. I was disillusioned to find that Dick Whittington was not a poor lad with a cat but obviously a crafty merchant in more ways than one. This did not stop me enjoying the pantomime, about my intellectual level, when it was shown at the Lyceum Theatre in the Strand.

In my last year at school we put on our own pantomime, Cinderella. Obviously in my opinion I was a natural for the part, but as I had a good pair of pins and a flat chest, I played Prince Charming. Who got the part of Cinderella? Jessie Hutchings, just because she had small feet! That's show business, folks!

CHAPTER
THREE

Hudsons and the Mating Game

I left school in the summer of 1925 at the age of fourteen with what was called an Elementary Education. I could read words of more than one syllable, write legibly and could cope with the rudiments of arithmetic. As my headmaster, tall, grey-haired, who ruled with an authority that needed no rod of iron, once remarked "Translate any problem into pounds, shillings and pence and Ethel will come up with the right answer even if she is only half-awake most of the time."

He was my father figure and I sat as near to him as possible, even though his false teeth would slip on occasions and spittle would bless my cheek like dew on an apple.

Nevertheless, I was glad to leave school and my first job required neither education nor intelligence. Mother decreed and I agreed, for it paid ten shillings a week.

I went to work in a factory filling bottles with Yeast Vite tablets. The hours were long and a photograph would have shown a shabby building in Clerkenwell with poorly dressed girls sitting at wooden benches. People looking at it today would say "Oh, what a shame". I didn't think so. I was earning money. I was warm and we chattered away like monkeys. I even put on weight! No-one, if memory serves me right, rebuked us or drove us along. I was always hungry, but at the same time felt intensely alive, quick on my feet and quick with my tongue. I couldn't match Mother's devastating repartee, but I was learning!

At dinner time we invariably pushed our way through Leather Lane Market where you could buy almost anything cheaply, some of it no doubt fallen off the back of a horse and cart. On one stall boiled sweets and toffee were made on the spot in large pans heated by naphtha gas. A treat for me was a dark red drink made from the root of a lily, deliciously cold in summer, blissfully hot in winter — Sarsaparilla! The name evoked images of proud Spanish dancers swirling to music played by copper-coloured fingers. The sweet smell of bubbling toffee, the scent of raspberry, strawberry, lemon, pineapple, orange from the boiled sweets newly set, all this plus bloater paste sandwiches and Sarsaparilla — magic!

Not far from the market were several streets of small houses mostly occupied by Italians and the area was known locally as Little Venice. Despite the occasional explosive quarrel, they were warm friendly people and on Feast Days would decorate their houses with flowers and bunting and most windows would have statuettes of Christ or the Virgin Mary in colours of gold, white and blue. Although sometimes solemn there was nothing sombre. All was colour and gaiety and I was happy with their happiness, just as delighted as they were by the processions of girls in their white dresses and veils on their way to church.

Some of these feasts went on for days and were so enjoyable that I considered becoming a Catholic. Apart from the imagined row with Mother which would be less than holy, I could not abandon my own truly loved St Clement Danes Church. Which was just as well, for I am sure that my old headmaster Mr Gerrard would not have approved and his approval turned out to be important.

I had been at the factory just under a year. On one glorious April evening I returned home to find a letter from Mr Gerrard who wrote that he had recommended me for the position of cashier at Hudson Brothers and would I please attend the interview he had arranged. He was confident of my success and so was I.

Mother gave her hard consent to the purchase of a new coat. New! I should be so lucky! The coat came after much searching through several jumble sales. It had been made from a multi-coloured blanket by someone who had no knowledge of buttons or button-holes. But it was in good nick and actually fitted. Not the usual "You'll grow into it" item. To my utter astonishment Mother, without being asked, forked out one shilling and eleven pence for a poke-bonnet style straw hat and another four pence for a bunch of artificial cherries for decoration! On the day of my interview I went out of my way to prance along the Strand to admire my reflection in the shop windows. Tap, tap, tap went my heels; click, click, click went the cherries. Oh elegant Ethel; oh pretty Miss Parker; how knowing but how naïve!

Hudson Brothers was on the corner of Maiden Lane and Bedford Street. Not a large shop but regarded as posh because it supplied top quality provisions to the Houses of Parliament, the Savoy Hotel and most of the gentlemens' clubs in Pall Mall. "Only the best quality for the best people," the manager informed me smugly when I finally met him. Before that however I was nearly thrown out of my stride by a newspaper seller literally falling at my feet as I approached the shop from Maiden Lane. He lay there foaming at the mouth, his body jerking convulsively. He was having a fit. Luckily other people knew him well, for it was no uncommon experience. With some relief I went into the shop to meet Mr Chiltern the manager.

Mr Chiltern was thin, dark, aged about thirty, with the head of a well groomed rat. He wore a distinctive dark blue coat to emphasize his authority. With an imperious wave of the hand I was beckoned into his office which was about the size of a large tea chest. He handed me a sheet of paper with columns of pounds, shillings and pence. "Add that," he said and leant back, but not for long. One eyebrow went up when I returned the paper and the other eyebrow rose when he checked the totals. "Good," he said, "that's quite good." Another paper followed for multiplication and division of money and the usual "how many for how much" type of problem. The eyebrows stayed down this time, but after another "Yes, quite good" and a few personal questions the job was mine for fifteen shillings a week.

I was sharp and streetwise but the manager was sharper and wiser. He got the best of the bargain. His air was self congratulatory as he introduced me to plump Miss Bevan who at fifty was quietly resigned to being an old maid. She was the book-keeper in charge of the office in which I was to work. This office was roughly equivalent to three tea-chests for there was also the ledger-clerk Miss Farquar, twenty, tiny, fair haired, happy. Her parents were caretakers for Moss Brothers and her father as a jazz clarinetist was quite popular. I was then introduced to Mr Joyce, the chief counter-hand, a healthy bright blue eyed man of about fifty who became my new father figure. The other four counter-hands and six store staff were ignored but I got to know them well in time.

When I came out of the shop, the newspaper seller was sitting on the pavement sorting out his papers, among which strutted a pigeon with the most beautiful ruff of blue and green, something of a contrast to the shabby black suit and cap of the man.

"He looks as if he's in charge," I said pointing to the pigeon.

"He's me mate, better than most, always comes dahn when I'm in trouble."

"Well, can I help?"

The man looked at the pigeon. The pigeon cocked an eye at me, plumped out his feathers and gave a deep-throated "coo — coo — coo". Taking that as a vote of confidence, I sorted out a few papers and asked "What's in the papers today anyway?"

"A load of bleedin' rubbish," was the reply.

"That makes a change for the better then," I said with a laugh.

And that's how I became a mate of "Arfer", but not of course equal to Charlie the pigeon. If Arthur didn't turn up, neither did Charlie.

"Where were you yesterday, Arthur?"

"Orspital."

"What happened?"

"You're all bleedin' questions! Parker's your right title, nosey ruddy Parker!"

I learnt some of the story as the months went past and I was able to cadge for him certain things like mittens, another muffler, bits and pieces of food to which even Mr Chiltern turned a blind eye.

Arthur had been wounded three times in the "War to end all Wars." The last wound was a "Blighty" one to the head. A piece of shrapnel had lodged near the brain and the surgeons had had to cut a piece of scalp away to get the metal out, but the brain was damaged, hence the fits and pitiful pension of ten shillings a week. Once when he was a bit groggy and delirious with cold Arthur showed me the metal plate which protected his head. It was covered with chamois leather and held in place with black elastic. It was about the size of the palm of my hand and the flesh underneath was patchy, wet and red. At the same time he began to talk of life in the trenches, not in a maudlin or boastful way but with such realism that I was there with him in the stinking mud, the rats, rotting limbs and the screaming shellfire.

Once, when he was bringing in a wounded man caught on the barbed wire, he fell into the trench with the man still on his back. The man was dead, hit by another bullet as Arthur was bringing him in.

"That bullet might have done for me if he 'adn't been on my back, poor sod."

Poor Arthur, he died soon after and I never found his grave; I didn't know his surname! Charlie never came back either.

When Arthur dismissed the newspapers as rubbish, he expressed the cynicism of many in Covent Garden who had become disillusioned with politics and politicians, but Mother was more vitriolic than ever about Churchill and that Welsh Whippet Lloyd George. She was equally scathing about the trade union leaders. For her it was Baldwin or the Bolsheviks and she was on the side of Baldwin. As I had heard all this before I took no notice, not realizing what was to come and how it was to affect my first day at Hudson Brothers.

The date was of some significance, Monday 3 May 1926, the first day of the General Strike. I arrived early, before eight a.m. and could hear the telephones ringing inside the store. Mr Chiltern, flushed and flustered, was also early. He threw open the door and strode from the butter counter to the cheese counter, from the ham counter to the coffee counter as he demanded theatrically of each new arrival, "How are we going to get supplies? How are we supposed to manage?"

I soon found that even in normal times Mr Chiltern was anxious and irritable for we had no refrigeration and demand had to be closely matched by supply. A dissatisfied customer would send Mr Chiltern into an extravagance of apology; a tart reminder from Head Office to keep no more than sufficient stock would send him into a rage. On this my first day he seemed to be in a continual frenzy, predicting riot, revolution, fire and famine.

Miss Farquar and I were inclined to giggle but were silenced by a solemn Miss Bevan. Even Mr Joyce looked troubled. The orders flooded in and I was kept very busy making out invoices and checking accounts. At dinner time I ran home, rushed up the stairs to pour out my version of the morning, but Mother was uncharacteristically quiet and paid no attention. Somewhat chastened I returned to work but was soon caught up in the renewed excitement.

In the evening I did a tour of the West End, just to watch and listen. People were arguing and gesticulating, some waving umbrellas and walking sticks at each other. I found it great fun, told Mother so and got a smart clip on the ear. My brother was hunched over his homemade crystal set and told me to shut up. Nevertheless I went to bed well satisfied with life.

I never ever rose like a lark, always clutched at the blanket "for just two more minutes", but on Tuesday, 4 May I awoke very early, awakened by of all things, the unnatural quiet. No shouts, no clatter of horses, no rattle of iron rims on cobble stones, no anything! Even Mother was quiet and went off to clean the offices at the Exchequer and Audit Department without her usual warnings of punishment for sins not yet committed.

By the time I reached Bedford Street the quiet was over, all was bedlam and confusion. People were getting to work by whatever means they could, on foot, by cycle or taxi, even on horseback. One man rode in on a farm horse which bolted over Waterloo Bridge which in common with the other bridges was jammed with cars, as were Marble Arch and Piccadilly.

All this I learnt during the morning from our agitated customers. As the days went by rumour fed upon rumour and the prophets of doom predicted the blood would run in the gutters. One morning Dr Ryan, who was attached to Bow Street police station, drew up in his gig, a very smart turnout all rich brown and brass. The pony was strong and stocky, chestnut coloured and immaculately groomed. The doctor, jovially tipsy as usual, strode into the shop and announced with great satisfaction, "I've patched a few heads this morning for sure, and where are me sage sausages?"

But I never saw any bloody encounters apart from the usual punch ups outside the pubs. There were certainly plenty of troops in battle dress and armoured cars driving up and down, but the people where I lived, far from looking for trouble, and whether belonging to a trade union or not, were bewildered and apprehensive, afraid of losing what little they had.

On the other hand our customers had no doubts; all strikers were traitors and criminals and should be shot.

Perversely the continuing crisis brought out the best in Mr Chiltern. With the help of the imperturbable Mr Joyce he acted with great assurance and controlled the greedy with phrases such as "take my advice, that lot won't keep" and "we guarantee fresh supplies in a day or so".

By Wednesday 5 May, Hudson Brothers had transport arranged to bring the staff into work and home again. I lived too close for that and felt I was missing out on much joking and laughter as the others clambered into the backs of lorries or horsedrawn carts. It was also arranged, sometimes with volunteers, for deliveries to the hotels, restaurants and clubs. One young man very posh in plus fours and a voice to match tried to deliver to the front entrance of the Savoy. Driving down the left side of Savoy Court he went smack into a limousine coming the other way. This caused much amusement to our staff, "Everyone knows that you drive on the right hand side down Savoy Court." Apparently it was the only street in England where this rule applied. Well, the young man didn't know and neither did I or Miss Farquar, but we admitted that only to each other.

I can remember nothing unusual about the weekend. My brother monopolized the crystal set. Mother was grim but still quiet. But by Monday the 10th the rumours were of buses and cars overturned, riots in the East End and baton charges by the police. Although I still did not understand what was at stake, that it wasn't just another great theatrical drama, I was relieved as anyone when it was over by the Thursday morning.

In a week or so life was almost normal. Mother was her old aggressive self again, Arthur had his old reluctant grin, Charlie cooing, Dr Ryan waving his long whip at me with a "Good morning to you, young Ethel," Mr Chiltern subservient and arrogant by turns.

Although I was often sarcastic behind his back, I realize now what a demanding job he had, balancing the requirements of customers, the harassment from Head Office, control of the staff, like the master of a three ring circus. He had to exercise quality control and credit control. Fine airs and graces were sometimes reluctant to pay bills and often affronted by even the politest reminder. No wonder the man lost his temper at times. I often wondered what effect it had on his family life.

My own home life changed little at first. My small attempts to brighten up the tenement were treated with indifference or derision. After my second or third week at Hudson's, coming home past the market on Saturday, I bought Mother a bunch of mixed flowers — mimosa, tulips and daffodils. She promptly threw them out of the window and boxed my ears for wasting money, my own money. I didn't cry, not then, not until I reached St James's Park, there I sobbed my heart out.

To the day she died Mother never lost the ability to hurt me. Nevertheless, I was changing in other ways; I was changing physically. I developed later than other girls of my age at school and like them was totally unprepared for the bodily and emotional changes of puberty.

Menstruation was unmentionable and I had never heard of sanitary towels. I wore a folded piece of cloth which had to be boiled, sterilized in salt and boiled again to get rid of the blood. Luckily, apart from the inconvenience, menstruation caused me no problems. I found it far harder to cope with my own increased sexuality. Masturbation was denounced as a vice but had the virtue of being private. I didn't know that it was practised the wide world over. To me it was a solitary sin and I alone was guilty. And, of course, an unwanted pregnancy was an economic and social calamity, to be avoided at all costs.

I never learned to play the mating game very well, and my first dates were disasters usually brought to an end by a clump of my handbag about the head of my equally inexperienced suitor. The mating game no longer matters now that I am a sweet tempered old lady, with white hair neatly set and dentures as firm as if fixed with glue. I smile at those who cod me with "How well you look!" and "How marvellous you are!" But I sometimes wonder why have I become so passive: why don't I spit in someone's eye?

Please, Lord, don't let me live to be witless, drooling and dribbling and fed from a spoon. Rather give me the courage to my own quietus make, to end my ways and days when and where I choose.

And I should like to round that end with a small achievement, something other than a tombstone to tell my story. Why have I left it so late? I don't know. After all, I was no fool. Uneducated and immature certainly, but not stupid. What went wrong?

Living so long in the dark shadow of Mother's drunkenness obviously did not help. Having my right leg partially severed by shrapnel; several operations for cancer; a dodgy heart; perhaps all these are part of the explanation. But there must have been more to it than that.

In 1926 at a time of mass unemployment, and the appalling degradation of the dole, was getting and keeping a job achievement enough in itself? Was I too happy at Hudson's? It was not well paid, but the people there became, as it were, my extended family. At last I belonged somewhere, was that it? And life at home did gradually change.

The tenement remained the same miserable brown job despite all my efforts, but we were all working and we kept out of debt. Mother moved up-market with her drinking. She went to Henekeys in the Strand and drank Guinness laced with port wine. She didn't seem to need so much to reach her happy, happy land of oblivion. Unless I was told that she was totally pie-eyed and incapable, I no longer went to bring her home; and she no longer woke me when she left at six a.m. At last I was getting reasonable hours of sleep and each morning went eagerly to work as once I had to the Market.

Our shop was ideally situated for its trade, better really than the Civil Service Stores directly opposite in Bedford Street. Hudson's faced north into Maiden Lane and only caught the afternoon sun in Bedford Street and then not for long. In summer it was a cool shop, important in days without refrigeration. In winter it was freezing. The floor and working surfaces for provisions were of fine cool marble. The other counters and woodwork were highly polished Spanish mahogany.

Mr Chiltern and I would arrive within seconds of each other, closely followed by the two cleaners, Doris and Elsie. Everyone was there by eight a.m. Lateness was a luxury not allowed. Doris was skinny with a melodious voice but only one tune, *Lily of Laguna*. Elsie was plump with bright brown eyes, a good bust and a well rounded bum which seemed to disturb Mr Chiltern's concentration when she was scrubbing the floor. Doris polishing the woodwork with the best wax excited no such attention except a request to "turn it down a bit". Although they had to work fast, they were very thorough and the place was kept scrupulously clean. Should Mr Chiltern find something to criticize, the two ladies would open their eyes in mock horror and together they would examine the offending blemish.

"There ain't nuffink there, Mr Chiltern!" And in a typical aside, "Spots before his eyes most like."

Nevertheless, the spot would be gone over again with exaggerated care. They would depart with "Hope you soon feel better, Mr Chiltern. Ta ta to everyone. See yer termorrer."

After Doris and Elsie had gone, we settled down to a slower but more methodical routine. Fresh supplies delivered by van were lowered through doors in the pavement to the very large stock room which was divided into smaller rooms, one for eggs, four separate ones for cheeses, another for hams and sides of bacon, another for chests of tea and sacks of coffee beans, and so on. Everything had to be in its place and kept strictly in its place. The seven men seemed happy enough in their catacombs, except for the egg chandler, a sad silent recluse who spent each and every day doing nothing but candle eggs. The war had left him with ruined lungs and he ate his lunch where he worked rather than make the painful climb up the stone stairs into the shop overhead.

Upstairs, apart from the predictable tantrums from Mr Chiltern, life was incredibly calm and relaxed. Where I sat I could see and hear almost everything. And I had plenty of time. As cashier I had only cash paying customers to worry about and they were comparatively rare. The bulk of the trade was with the better restaurants and hotels, Rules, the Savoy, the Ritz for example. They had special and varying rates of credit and their accounts would be kept by Marjorie Farquar and Jessie Bevan. Each morning I had time to watch Mr Parry and Mr Joyce start their day by dressing their windows and counters. Each was an artist, Mr Parry with provisions, Mr Joyce with groceries.

On the provisions side, York hams, black Bradenham hams, fat succulent hams, tender lean hams, the first on tall china stands; whole sides of bacon, gammon, hocks, half sides of bacon cut to show the back and collar. There were all sizes of pork pies and variously flavoured sausages. But it was with the cheeses that Mr Parry excelled. Every day a new masterpiece of cream, yellow, orange and brown, with that important touch of blue.

Whole Cheddars and Cheshires, half Cheddars and Cheshires, strong, mild or medium, wedges, oblongs, rounds, offset by creamy or blue veined Stiltons and Gorgonzolas; Dutch and Edam in their red skins side by side with the intriguing Gruyère and the hard-hearted expensive Parmesan.

Like Mr Parry, Mr Joyce was an artist but more restrained in style. In the centre of his counter were a pair of finely wrought highly polished brass scales. On his right were samples of top quality coffee beans in porcelain dishes, on his left a selection of the wide range of expensive teas available. To add colour were small boxes of glacé fruits and small jars of fancy preserves. That was all. On request, however, he could produce any type of biscuit from the glass topped boxes behind him; and from the small bank of drawers samples of nuts — whole almonds, skinned, split, chopped, ground almonds, brazil nuts, walnuts, pistachio nuts, coconut desiccated or in strips, chestnuts; samples of spice — mace, whole nutmegs, peppercorns, white pepper, black pepper, paprika, oregano, cinnamon, ginger, cayenne, turmeric. All the sugars, cereals, flour and legumes were kept in sacks in the store below.

Mr Parry was small, slim, fastidious, with a pale intelligent face and brown eyes. Mr Joyce was taller, plumper and had a clear complexion and blue eyes. They were both kind, cheerful and totally professional, deferential but not obsequious towards the customers.

There was one more counter. This was devoted entirely to butter and the formidable Miss Palmer. She was dressed like a dairy maid and had ruddy cheeks and fair hair. But she was built and worked like a navvy, slamming and throwing the butter about all day, hundredweights of it made up into pats with the special crest of the especial customers on them. Both Miss Palmer and Miss Bevan ignored the current fashion for women to appear flat-chested, and their ample bosoms were unconfined. They seemed serenely unaware of the effect their softly bouncing breasts were having on the men, particularly on our two salesmen, Mr Warren and Mr Gillett whose job it was to drum up trade from the clubs, hotels and restaurants.

They came in each morning with their orders from the previous day and to agree with Mr Chiltern terms of credit or discount. Again Hudson Brothers had chosen winners, they were both good looking, amusing, intelligent and had served with some distinction in the war. They had incredible memories, and could discuss each client's pet loves or hates, their anniversaries and even children's birthdays. They must have been on first name terms with half the chefs in London. Mr Gillett took particular pleasure on checking his customers accounts and admiring Miss Bevan's deep cleavage at the same time. I would get a hug and a kiss on the cheek, but my flat chest evoked no interest whatsoever.

I was, however, becoming increasingly aware that I had a good pair of legs and felt a certain embarrassed pleasure when I had to go down the stairs into the store. The men invariably paused to watch me and I should have been disappointed it they hadn't. By this time I was physically and emotionally attracted to older men like Mr Parry and Mr Joyce, enjoyed the warmth of their arm about my waist, was totally at ease with them, but in no way associated them with my private fantasies.

Luckily for me I seemed to arouse only paternal and protective feelings in them. Had they attempted any further intimacy my happy world at Hudsons would have crashed about my ears. There I felt safe and secure. Male and female created He them and where two or three are gathered together, male and female are physically aware of this, consciously or unconsciously. It adds that something extra to the atmosphere even where, as at Hudsons, it was kept strictly under control.

It was due to their encouragement, Mr Parry, Mr Joyce and Miss Bevan, that I began a course in book-keeping. Began but never finished, I pursued it ineffectually for six months and was bored beyond belief. I changed over to dress-making which liberated all my creative energy and imagination. This was one of those moments which taken at the flood might have led to fame and fortune. I had a natural flair for design and my experiments with cheap bright material from Berwick Market earned me the nickname of Jazzy. Whatever the reason, ignorance, stupidity or just plain happiness, I did not realize the commercial potential of what I was doing and was deeply satisfied with making my own clothes and those of a few friends. Of course I had the advantage of Mother's sewing machine, which was still not paid for.

It was at these classes that I met another Maud, or Maudie as she was called. She was a year or so older than me and she had what the boys wanted, a sexy figure, always good for a kiss and a cuddle and ready to laugh at their jokes. She also undertook my education in the gentle art of courting and the more strenuous activity of heavy petting, for this was a time when boys and girls hunted in pairs. Unfortunately I was reluctant to pursue and when pursued inclined to flight or fight. Maudie was pretty with good teeth, naturally blonde hair and a body plump with promise. I was good looking enough, proud of my legs but promised nothing.

We usually went for the clerical type. They were at least reasonably dressed even if they were hard up and wc had to pay for our own coffee. The meetings usually took place in a Lyons tea shop, where we played the young ladies about town lark, nonchalantly sipping our coffee and trying not to choke over our first cigarette. The cigarette caper was a recognized excuse for an introduction. A coquettish "Have you a match?" led to some inane reply, false laughter and a shuffling around of chairs.

Then we all went for a stroll, usually the park and back along the Strand to find convenient doorways for a goodnight kiss and cuddle. I was as pliant and yielding as a poker and my partners soon gave up. We never allowed them, they seldom offered, to see us home, for Maudie lived in Peabody Buildings in Drury Lane which were worse than Stirling Buildings. On the way home Maudie would scold me for being uncooperative which made me morose and miserable.

However, one evening we struck lucky, even the short one was good looking and they bought coffee and cakes. Although a head taller than Herbie I managed to be less awkward at the petting game and we spent many pleasant times together. We arranged to meet one summer evening on the Embankment. I was proud of my new outfit I had made, almost an exact copy of one in Bond Street. I had silk stockings, a new pair of good shoes and a bra padded with cotton wool. I was, I assured myself, a peach, a stunner, a consort fit for a prince.

It was no prince that I met. Herbie's suit was all right, but he had two black eyes, a split lip and a conk like a squashed beetroot. Yet he and his mate seemed pleased with themselves and greeted us with smiles. I noticed Herbie was missing one front tooth. I was both shocked and concerned. What on earth could have happened? Herbie looked down modestly at his feet while his mate explained. Herbie was a promising light-weight boxer and the previous night had defeated one of the best in London. Defeated! What did the other bloke look like, for God's sake! I tried to accept the situation, although people turned to look at us wherever we went. By the time we came to say goodnight I was solicitude itself. I kissed his tender swollen lips gently and warmly. Herbie emboldened by his victory the night before, decided to press for another one. To my utter astonishment he took my hand and closed it around his penis. His nose took the full force of my handbag and he let out a howl that set the dogs barking for miles around. I did not wait for Maudie.

When we met later she was furious. "You should have seen the blood he lost! His suit's ruined, you know." Apparently there was a myth among men that a woman would swoon with delight when she held a man's penis. And after all, Maudie said, it only needed a few supple movements of the wrist and the man's ardour was satisfied and the woman's prestige and honour preserved. Not so bloody likely, mate. I wasn't trying that one. Our friendship and my instruction ended there and then.

I went to work next morning somewhat subdued, only to suffer more when Mr Harvey of Moët and Chandon walked in. He was tall, about forty, handsome, courteous, impeccably dressed with beautiful shoes. He was straight out of one of my fantasies. A kiss from him and my virtue would have been undone. Just to hear his voice turned me on. I went hot all over when he came to my desk and said, "Hello, Ethel. I saw you last evening. Your young man had taken quite a battering. Not by you I hope."

I vehemently explained that Herbie was not my young man, not then, never had been or ever would be. I floundered on and on, making matters worse and worse. Others, particularly Jessie and Marjorie, were listening with increasing interest, so I finally excused myself, fled to the loo and had a good cry.

When I finally emerged from the loo, my embarrassment was disregarded. Mr Harvey in conversation with Mr Parry paused to give me a friendly smile. Mr Joyce was engaged with Mr and Mrs Eustace Miles. Miss Palmer was knocking hell out of the butter, Jessie and Marjorie asked me to give them a hand with some invoices. I felt grateful to them all, even to Mrs Eustace Miles whose sweet voice like a clear English brook burbled on and on and on. She was very tall and, conscious of a slight resemblance to Queen Mary, tried to dress the part with a toque hat, longish skirts, high heeled shoes and a rolled umbrella to match. She and poor old Eustace Miles sat in chairs facing each other. He, short and fat, said nothing but nodded his head up and down like a mechanical doll, while she trilled and thrilled about her latest creation. Although she was a pain, Mr Joyce treated her with respect for she was probably the finest vegetarian cook in London and their restaurant in Chandos Street was deservedly successful. They were also prompt in settling their account.

This account in no way compared to that of Moët and Chandon who had an impressive building in Northumberland Avenue and who obviously entertained on a lavish scale. Only the very best of the best was good enough for them and Mr Harvey was a connoisseur whose approval was valued for its own sake by those three professionals, Messrs Chiltern, Parry and Joyce. He was also generous and gave gifts to us all at Easter and Christmas.

Another customer who was appreciated for his own sake was Mr Bell of Rules Restaurant in Maiden Lane. He seemed to be always happy and smiling and had good reason to be. Rules was the "in place" for writers and actors. Novello went there regularly and, worse luck, so did Olivia Burleigh. According to grandfather, Rules was renowned even in his day when the lovers of literature and the stage might, repeat might, after dining like dukes, tip like princes. No matter how famous the person, by grandfather's standards people were only as good, bad or indifferent as the size of their tips. Dickens did not rate highly on that scale, but once parted with a sovereign in mistake for a shilling. Grandmother got her housekeeping money that week.

"Give him his due," said grandfather, "Dickens would have made a damned good cabbie. You couldn't take him the long way round, he knew the streets backwards."

Mr Bell used to appear about lunchtime (we called it dinner) when I was already ravenous from the smell of the hams, the cheeses, especially the pungent appetizing Camembert, mixed with the aroma of the coffees freshly roasted and ground to order right there in the shop by Mr Joyce. Mr Bell lounging at ease in one of the many chairs sometimes described in detail an extravagant dinner served the night before and I could feel myself getting thinner and thinner, my cheeks pinched and white with starvation and envy.

Yet to be honest we were eating better at home. I was as tall as Mother now and although threatened often enough there were no more clips on the ear. Our verbal battles however were frequent and explosive and at times I won. I sometimes deliberately provoked her with for example, "Nancy Astor is giving a talk on the evils of drink. You ought to go, you might get converted."

The very mention of Nancy Astor was enough to send Mother straight to the pub, but I was adamant that with every increase in wage, my money had to be spent on food and not on booze. Mother even began to come home midday to cook a proper meal, although it was often accompanied by "I hope that will suit madam" as she slapped my plate down in front of me. When I told her she was a great cook she sniffed contemptuously, but spoilt the effect by a look of smug satisfaction. If she should be out at work I usually made myself an omelette or a salad.

On one such day I was badly shaken to find Herbie barring the stairs. He didn't say a word, just glared and refused to let me pass. I was about to turn and run when Ginger Tom came along. He glanced at us both, put one great arm affectionately about Herbie's shoulders, congratulated him on his boxing and drew him out on to the street. I could not hear what was said, but Tom appeared to be amiability itself. They finally shook hands and Herbie went off with a bit of a swagger in his walk.

"What did you say to him?" I asked Tom. He gave me a hug and sat me down on the stairs behind him.

"I told him yer mum was a right old cow who would have his guts for garters, and she has a lot of mates among the 'eavy mob in the Market."

"Thank you, Tom," I said and gave him a peck on the cheek.

"I also sed as how you was tuppence short of a shilling and shouldn't be let out on yer own. I sed as how he was too good a bloke to waste his time on a skirt like you."

"Thank you for bloody nothing!" I said and tried to get up.

"Don't be so bleedin' daft, Ethel. It's time you grew up. You ought not to lead blokes on and then belt them with yer handbag! A bit of buttering up never hurt nobody. If yer don't like a bloke, don't come the madam, but let 'im down gentle and easy like. We've all got our pride, yer know."

"You've got what!" said a voice above us. There was Ivy. She was shaking with anger. "You silly old bugger, cuddling in public on your own doorstep and her showing her legs off up to her bum."

I stood up in a hurry, Tom quite slowly. Ivy continued to rave, but Tom, his chubby face set like stone, told her to "Shut it, Duchess." She shut it. He picked her up like a rag doll and started up the stairs.

I tried to speak but was told to "Hop it!" I hopped it.

CHAPTER
FOUR

Thinking It Out Again

I spent the afternoon in misery, wondering whether Ivy was getting beaten up, and what to do if Mother got to know about it. After work I walked slowly home still unable to think clearly. Even more slowly I walked up the stairs to Tom and Ivy's tenement and knocked on the door. I had difficulty in breathing. Ivy opened the door. Her face relaxed into a warm, welcoming smile.

"Come in, luv! Tom's up Berwick Market. He won't be back for a bit."

I could not believe it! Her hair was dressed up and she looked radiant.

"Come on in," she said, "I won't bite."

"About this morning, Ivy," I began.

"Forget it Ethel. But Tom's right yer know. If you start acting like that tart Maudie, you'll get treated like a tart. And if you keep belting blokes, one day you'll get belted back."

I was shaken. "How do you know so much about it?"

"Be yer age, luv. The Strand's not in Siberia and people aren't blind."

I felt hot, ashamed and confused. God, I thought, Mother must know! My emotions boiled over into tears and I sat in Ivy's kitchen like a clumsy oversized schoolgirl being lectured by a diminutive head teacher. Showing too much leg came into it, of course, but it was a shock to learn that I had the habit of leaning up against older men. It was all a question of being choosy, clean and attractive and waiting until the right man came along.

"How am I to know, and what if he doesn't come along?"

"Then it's your hard luck, ducky and you'll either have to go without, or make the best of what's left over."

Then she complimented me on my dressmaking and explained how she made the most of a particular actress's figure.

"She's like you," she said, "She's got no tits either."

"Thank you, Ivy," I said. "You're doing me the world of good. The tart with no tits. Are you sure you haven't missed anything out?"

Ivy rocked with laughter and as she recrossed her legs I noticed that she was wearing a pair of lacy black knickers; this was a day of revelation indeed!

Before I could think of a question leading to knickers, Tom came bouncing in. He handed Ivy a small parcel with a bow, "There you are, Duchess," and then he picked me up and swung me above his head.

Ivy smiling indulgently said, "Put her down, Tom, stop showing off."

She tore open the parcel and there was a jade, at least it looked like jade, necklace. She held it out for Tom to fasten it about her thin throat. His large arms

95

closed about her little body, and I closed the door behind me. I doubt whether they noticed.

I walked thoughtfully down to our tenement. Mother was obviously at Henekeys; where Bill was I neither knew nor cared. I lay on the bed I shared with Mother and tried to imagine Tom's heavy naked body on top of frail Ivy. Then it occurred to me, perhaps she was on top. I'd never heard of such a thing, but I supposed it possible! One thing was for sure, tomorrow was another day and I would have to start playing the mating game by a different set of rules.

Despite of, or because of, a night made restless by dreams, I was up early the next morning and walked down Savoy Hill to the Embankment, across the tramlines and as far as Cleopatra's Needle. The tide was in and the clouds piling up from the west were lit up by the opposing sun. The river was busy with noisy tugs towing long lines of rusty barges. A police launch was going full tilt towards Westminster Bridge. I sniffed the smokey air and felt great.

The conductor of a stationary tram blew me a kiss. To hell with it, I thought, and blew a kiss back. I turned up Northumberland Avenue, into the Strand and along to Hudson Brothers and hopefully a cuddle from Mr Joyce or Mr Parry, or both. It wasn't a sexual need (is that Freud laughing?), but more a reassurance of the affection I wanted.

Nevertheless, I had decided on certain changes — to be more restrained in style and colour of dress, to wear longer skirts, to be more circumspect in descending and ascending the store room stairs, to accept Marjorie

Farquar's often repeated invitations to attend whist drives and socials given by Harry Moss to his employees and their friends.

Moss Brothers was a splendid shop in Bedford Street with plenty of window space for men's wear, for suits, shirts and hats for all occasions — weddings, funerals, business, leisure, even for hunting the fox — all to be had on hire. The shop inside was handsomely furnished with changing rooms, large mirrors and comfortable chairs. The staff were well trained, well dressed, courteous, attentive and, it appeared, contented.

To start with I went home with Marjorie to have tea and learn whist from her and her parents. Mrs Farquar was Irish with beautiful brown eyes, a lovely complexion and a soft accent that made the most ordinary words sound like music. Mr Farquar had a knee shattered by shrapnel and, like Cap, walked with a sideways swoop. Unlike Cap there was nothing sinister or violent about him. He was truly a gentle man, with a love of jazz, particularly the playing of Johnny Dodds and Sidney Bechet. Marjorie, taking after her parents, was attractive, self-contained, good humoured and with a laugh soft and musical like her mother's. I had rarely been at such ease with anyone before.

But I found all the staff at Moss Bross easy to get on with, and I particularly enjoyed the Friday evening whist drives. The counters were cleared to one side to make room for the green baize topped tables, and a buffet set up at one side for refreshment halfway through the evening. There were usually forty or more players, some of them young men, some not so young whose attentions, following Marjorie's example, I was able to accept gracefully.

I went to the cinema and the music hall with first one then another, but however much my body craved love, my intellect said, "Not this one, Ethel." I always acted with the greatest decorum, thanked them warmly for a marvellous evening and bade them goodnight just as a convenient bus or tram came along. You could rely on public transport in those days. It was my hard luck if the bus or tram was going in the wrong direction, but it was a wonderful technique, even if the prim and proper Miss Parker rarely got asked out twice by the same man.

People talk of double standards, the difference between public and private morality. Some maintain that the difference is necessary for the greater good of society. But it infuriated me that with sexual standards, in the working class at least, it was the man who got the pleasure and the woman who got the blame. According to some newspapers of the time, women of the "upper set", the cream of society, could do as they pleased provided they did not frighten the horses. Not so in Covent Garden. If a girl had intercourse outside marriage she was a whore and a slut, while the man was a gay dog doing what came naturally. At the same time those same newspapers, and some men, were conducting a hate campaign against Marie Stopes for advocating birth control education. Give Mother her due, she was on the side of Marie Stopes, though she was probably on the side of Herod as well.

It was Jessie Bevan who introduced me to the ideas of Marie Stopes. Jessie wasn't quite the staid old maid she appeared to be. Marjorie, who would have been content in a nunnery, had gently chided me for a cuddle more affectionate than usual with Mr Joyce. Jessie looking up from her ledger had said, "Oh Marjorie, don't be so prudish! They weren't exactly copulating behind the counter!"

I had not heard of copulating before and needed further explanation much to Jessie's amusement and Marjorie's embarrassment. The phrase "copulating behind the counter" had a good round sound to it and I rolled it round my tongue several times that afternoon just to annoy Marjorie. I thought that would put my Friday evenings up the spout but she was as generous as she was good and I went to tea with her that evening as usual and thought I was foolish to put such pleasure in jeopardy.

An additional advantage was the opportunity to know Jessie much better, and we began to walk together first by one route and then another to her railway station. Some evening before going home she had her tea at a Lyons and went on to a lecture or meeting. That is how I went with her to Walworth to hear Marie Stopes. It led on to an astonishing argument between Jessie and myself. Marie Stopes was all for birth control within marriage. Jessie was all for birth control, and getting to know someone over breakfast before marriage. At her age! I was appalled and got thoroughly trapped in my own prejudices and confusions.

I promised not to repeat our conversations to anyone else, a promise I kept until now. Eventually I found the courage to use the word masturbation and self-abuse.

"Self-abuse nothing!" said Jessie in a voice loud and clear as we were having tea in Lyons. The chatter and the clatter ceased as if brimstone had suddenly erupted from the spout of every teapot and the Day of Judgement was at hand. I did my best to hide behind the menu.

"Self-abuse," said Jessie with even greater emphasis, "is a load of . . ." she hesitated, "is a load of poppycock. Masturbation is self-love, and if you don't love yourself no-one else will. Realize that and it won't bother you half so much."

And she was right, it became no longer a constant guilty preoccupation and when I made love to myself I did so without shame.

Having received absolution from my sins in a Lyons Tea Shop, I went back to St Clement Danes Church with a sense of renewal, to enjoy again the ritual of prayer and hymn in that lovely building with its high, richly decorated ceiling, its choir and its very, very special Flowers Sellers Shrine. I tried other churches, even the Scottish National Church, the one that is curiously interlocked with the Fortune Theatre in Russell Street, but always returned to St Clement Danes with a sense of coming home.

The next two or three years were relatively happy for me. I was totally content at Hudson Brothers, too content, I realize now and, unknown to Mother, turned down better paid jobs just to stay there. I became a dab hand at whist, although the prizes I won were derided and devalued by Mother. For want of practice I became only marginally better at the mating game. I was grateful, but obviously not grateful enough, for it didn't happen often that I was taken to the cinema, a dance or the Holborn Empire. The expected goodnight kiss could be agreeable and if the man derived pleasure from caressing a pad of cotton wool, that was fine with me, but if his hands should move towards my thighs, my legs would lock together so tightly that Jupiter would have broken a wing trying to prize them apart. There was nothing I could do about it, it just happened. I did my best to let the man down "gentle and easy like" as advised by Tom, with delicate hints to the time of the month as suggested by Ivy and Jessie. If that didn't work, it was back to the bus or tram routine.

With Ivy's help I became even more proficient at making my own clothes, less gaudy in colour and more classical in style. We spent many Sunday evenings together, going over patterns, combining one with another, creating new ones entirely. My padded bras had to be particularly well constructed for with heavy handed males like Tom they were quickly knocked out of shape. Having gracefully extricated oneself from an amorous encounter, it was disconcerting to board a bus with a lop-sided bosom. Many years later padded bras were all the rage and could be bought over the counter, but were expensive. If only Ivy and I had had the entrepreneurial skills, the commercial know-how, we could have anticipated the bosom boom and made a lot of money.

We were a good team, Ivy with her years of experience and me with the imagination of youth and Mother's sewing machine. I used to buy sixpenny patterns from Weldons in Wellington Street and from them make something fashionable but different and individual. Time and time again I was stopped in the street with, "Excuse me, dear, where did you buy your dress?" Ivy ignored fashion altogether and wore simple straight dresses that made her look young for her age and, although thin, she was not frail. She had a grip like a steep clamp and was rarely ill. But one bleak February Monday, as I was about to go to work, a neighbour stopped me to say that Ivy wanted to see me.

I went up and when she opened the door her pale face was flushed and her hair uncombed. She had a towel wrapped round her.

"I think I've got flu, Ethel. Be a dear, get me some aspirins."

Now influenza in those days was no joke. People had not forgotten the epidemic of 1919. Thousands had died from it, particularly among the poor.

"First things first," I said. "Let's get you into bed."

I found her a flannelette nightdress and took the towel from her.

Hers was the first naked body I had seen and I looked at her in amazement. Her tiny figure was perfect, firm and supple as a ballerina. Wet with sweat it glistened like polished ivory.

"Ivy, you're so beautiful!"

She managed a grin. "So Tom keeps telling me."

With a sense of awe I wiped the sweat from her face and body, helped her with her nightdress and into bed. As I went down stairs I marvelled at what I had seen. The expression "an old head on young shoulders" was literally true in Ivy's case.

Mother was back from the Exchequer and Audit and looked a bit done in. She straightened herself up when she saw me and wanted to know what the bloody hell I was playing at. I explained briefly. Without another word she jammed her hat like a battle helmet back on her head, took the blankets from our bed, produced half a bottle of whisky and marched upstairs. When I returned with the aspirins, the kettle was on and Ivy was protesting in vain that she did not like whisky. I was told to "bugger off back to work".

Mr Chiltern began to upbraid me as soon as I entered the shop. Mr Harvey was there cool and elegant as always and I felt both humiliated and angry. Controlling my temper I asked to see Mr Chiltern in his office, sat down unbidden and very, very quickly explained about Ivy. If Mr Chiltern wanted my notice I could write it out for him there and then. He sat there silent for some moments, rubbing his fingers backwards and forwards against his forehead. He reached into a drawer and brought out a sepia photograph of a handsome woman holding a small boy in her arms.

"My wife and son," said Mr Chiltern. "They died from influenza in 1918 while I was still in France."

"Oh God," I thought, "I've done it again."

Judge not others lest you yourself by judged. How often I had made cheap and shoddy remarks about his home life.

"No-one else in the shop knows this," he said, "and I trust you not to tell them. I shall tell Miss Bevan that you are taking a day from your holiday, but," he held up his hand as I started to thank him, "do not threaten me with your notice again for I shall accept it. These are hard times, Ethel, labour is cheap, there are a lot of yesterday's heroes walking the streets out there. Right, off you go, make arrangements for your friend, but don't be late tomorrow."

I left his office, waved a hand at the others and walked conscience-stricken into the thin cold rain of Maiden Lane. What arrangements were needed, Mother had made. She had ambushed Dr Ryan who had endorsed her prescription for aspirin and whisky. She had sent for Tom, alerted Mrs Hutchings and others, and gone on to Lincolns Inn Fields. Tom sat by the bed wiping Ivy's face as she lay gently snoring, Mrs Hutchings was brewing more tea. Feeling a little piqued at losing my role of Florence Nightingale, I left them to it.

In Drury Lane for two shillings I bought a fat rabbit which the butcher skinned, gutted and cut into pieces. Back at home I stoked up the fire and prepared a rabbit stew for dinner. When Mother came stomping in, cold and wet, having satisfied herself that I had not got the sack, she changed her clothes and slumped in front of the fire without a word of complaint. I realized she was getting older and felt a pang of pity, which was premature for she continued to play merry hell for another twenty-six years.

Ivy was just as indomitable. In two days, though shaky on her pins, she was back at work. Mother received most of the credit plus a full bottle of whisky from Tom. My reward was a kiss and a hug from Ivy. The memory of her perfect little body disturbed me for some time and I now wonder whether, had I been born into a different class or at a different time, I might have become a lesbian. I doubt it. I knew nothing of homosexuality, never heard of it, which was just as well.

The mating game was complicated enough as it was. For at that time there was a gentleman, note the word "gentleman", whose attentions were giving me much cause for thought.

We met at a dance at Moss Bros. I was twenty, he was in his mid-thirties. He was tall, but not handsome, his jowl was heavy and dark, tufts of hair sprouted from his nose and ears but, having been a wallflower for two dances, I would have gladly waltzed with Mr Hyde. I avoided looking up his nose and concentrated on the quality of his clothes and his small elegantly shod feet. We danced and talked, we danced again and talked some more. He was a salesman for a textile company in Bradford.

"Call me Sam," he said. "Everyone calls me Sam, because my name is Weller."

The significance of that escaped me; I assumed it must have something to do with Yorkshire. When he asked me to dine the next evening at Lyons Corner House at Marble Arch, I trod on his foot, swallowed hard, trod on his other foot and said in accents wild, "Why not?"

I had second thoughts when he asked what time he should call for me, so I told him bluntly about Mother and the tenement.

"What's new?" he asked. "I was born in a back to back. Will seven o'clock be all right for you?"

I watched him arrive by taxi. He looked very, very prosperous. I did not hurry to open the door. Let the neighbours have a good look, I thought. My appearance obviously pleased him. My dress was elegant, simple, dove grey. I wore no jewellery. He helped me on with my coat which was wool, classic in cut and a lovely shade of green. My hat with its foot high plume was a perfect match. Cool and composed I took his arm and walked down the stairs, smack into Ginger Tom.

"Blimey," he said as I stuck out my tongue. Then as we passed, the bugger called out, "Watch out for her handbag, guvnor!"

The Corner House in those days was very plush with lots of gold paint, chandeliers and an orchestra. There were even carpets in the loo which was all artificial marble and coloured porcelain. The food wasn't bad either. When we sat down at our table, reserved of course, I said "yes" to everything Sam suggested, refusing only the wine. I was so famished I would have eaten the tablecloth had it been edible. We didn't say much as we steadily worked our way through the menu, but over coffee and cigarettes we talked, or rather (one of the rules of the mating game) he talked and I listened about the mills and moors of Yorkshire. I looked the other way while he paid the bill. He obviously tipped to everyone's satisfaction for they hoped they would see us again, and so did I.

The night air was crisp. The high clouds playing conjuring tricks with a thin moon. We took a bus to Regent Street, then walked arm in arm to Piccadilly Circus, down Haymarket to Pall Mall and on to the Strand. I foolishly told him about the Market at night. He wanted to see and hear for himself the strange shapes like crouching animals, the sudden snap and flap of a tarpaulin tugged by the wind. Too late I realized no buses were on hand in the deserted Piazza but he didn't even put his arm around my waist. He was more interested in the glass roof of the Floral Hall. I was still somewhat bemused when he escorted me to my door, thanked me for a grand evening, lightly kissed my cheek and said goodnight.

And that remained the pattern of our relationship. He wrote a short friendly letter when he was coming to London. We then met, dined and walked miles through the narrow alleys and squares of Westminster and the City.

One Saturday afternoon we went to a small tea shop in the Strand, run by two young ladies who had a small account with Hudson Brothers. Their arrival at our shop tended to disrupt our normally leisurely pace. They used to bounce in, breasts bobbing and bottoms wobbling in unison. They always dressed gaily and whirled from counter to counter like demented dragonflies whose day was about to end. Their order given, they departed arm in arm, skirts going swish-swish from side to side.

The interior of their shop was dimly lit, with mahogany cubicles curtained off from the serving area. It was the perfect rendezvous for covert courtship, for holding hands and declarations of illicit passion. I thought it very romantic. Sam was moved too; he said the pastries were nearly as good as those in Harrogate.

While admitting that he aroused little passion in me, it was galling that I appeared to arouse none in him. He was affectionate but avuncular. This variant of the mating game baffled not only me, but Ivy and Jessie as well. Jessie was all for more provocative action, Ivy for caution. Mother and I had bitter quarrels about Sam. She was certain that he was a twicer and not to come home crying to her if I ended up in the family way.

"Chance would be a fine thing. He hasn't even kissed me on the lips yet," I retorted.

"Bloody fool," she said, "That proves there's something wrong with him."

To be honest I preferred things as they were. I enjoyed the meals, the walks, the one or two visits to the theatre. We had seats in the stalls for *The Song of the Drum*, another lavish production at Drury Lane and that was followed by *The Land of Smiles* with Richard Tauber. I was grateful and said so, I didn't have to pretend anything else. I never told Mother that she was nearly right.

At the end of June 1932 Sam gave me a present for my birthday.

"But my birthday isn't until July, Sam."

"I know, but I won't be here then. This is a goodbye present as well. Textiles are finished in this country. I'm going to America and taking my wife and children with me."

I stood and thought for a moment.

"Sam," I said, "Could we go for a meal, I'm starving."

We ended where we began, in the Corner House at Marble Arch. It was a splendid meal. I had two helpings of nearly everything. I even drank champagne to the health of his family and their prosperity in America.

How does the song go? —

> "I got high as a steeple
> But we were intelligent people.
> No tears, no fuss,
> Hooray for us.
> Awfully glad I met you.
> Cheerio and toodle-oo!
> Thanks for the memory."

We parted in Oxford Street. I walked carefully but happily down Bond Street, almost straight into the arms of Henry.

Henry was a journalist, six foot four inches tall, skinny with a mop of straw coloured hair and very large hands and feet. He was a very earnest young man believing passionately in free love and communism and had an unlimited capacity for making a fool of himself. He could trip over a kerb that wasn't there and walk into a lamp post that was. When I was about eighteen and he twenty-two, Henry wanted to do the honourable thing, not marry me, but relieve me of my virginity in a comfortable bed rather than a shop doorway.

Our last meeting had been appropriately a farce at the Aldwych. During the interval, having caused some disturbance in getting to and from the bar, he leant nonchalantly against the wall and set off the fire alarm. In the ensuing furore, people got rather excited, I had a fit of the giggles and we were put out into the Strand. Henry had tried to appeal to the commissionaire as a comrade, but he, preferring to be a capitalist lackey, told us to bugger off. Later that evening I told Henry to do something similar and he walked bandy-legged into the sunset, a cowboy whose gun had gone off at half-cock.

I had not seen him since. But here he was in Bond Street, embracing me and knocking my hat askew in the same old way. His obvious admiration compensated for the vanishing euphoria of the champagne and I agreed to see him again.

In 1932, the textile trade was not the only industry in trouble, most of them were. Yesterday's heroes were being further degraded by the Means Test which took away the remnants of their pride and left them begging in the gutter. The old music hall song *While London Sleeps* said it all:

There's a lot of wealth and happiness in London,
There's lots of starving misery as well.
There's people good and true
Who can't get work to do . . .

I was one of the lucky ones. I had taken over Marjorie Farquar's job. She had defected to Harrods which Mr Chiltern bitterly described as a "palatial marble hall filled with rubbish". Little else had changed at Hudson's. We had a new cashier, a prim Miss Jones. And we were all six years older. We still sold the best quality to the best people and even the sale of a pound of butter had to be recorded in triplicate. To me it was a haven of calm in a world of confusion.

Outside there were so many different voices, so many prescriptions for paradise, always tomorrow. They had one theme in common, our present woes were all the fault of Ramsay Macdonald. Mother called him, and Ramsay Mac himself agreed with her, "a Scottish socialist bastard". It was said that he carried his birth certificate to remind himself of his illegitimate birth in a two-roomed shack among the smell of horse shit.

Henry being Henry managed at one and the same time to be a pacifist, a communist and work for the *Daily Mail*. As Maudie all those years before had undertaken my sexual education, so now Henry undertook my political education, with more or less the same result, total confusion on my part. We went to innumerable meetings, talks and lectures. The pacifists abused one another. The socialists and communists were forever passing resolutions and ultimatums condemning each other. History was supposed to be on someone's side, but I can't remember whose. I agreed with Mother that Nancy Astor was a pain in the arse and Wells fluting away wasn't much better.

It was a relief to enjoy the uncomplicated pleasure of window shopping in the West End with Ivy on a Sunday afternoon or evening. She was great fun to be with, full of stage gossip and a wicked eye for fancy underwear. I used to make rough sketches of the more classical expensive clothes, the inset of a sleeve, that type of thing. The styles were not too difficult. The problem was trying to match the quality of the material.

I was still friends with Marjorie Farquar, going to whist drives and dances with her, and I helped to make some of her clothes. Together we scoured the markets, particularly Berwick Market, for affordable material. This is where we both missed Sam for he had given us several lengths of fine worsted which I was able to make up into suits.

With Henry there was no material or posh meals. His job, so he assured me, entailed the frequent frequenting of pubs to mix with the doyens of his trade. He could, so he said, introduce me to A, B, and C. As I was not particularly interested in A, B, or C, and pubs were anathema to me anyway, the end of my political education was predictable.

What I had not foreseen was that it would end abruptly on the top of a number eleven bus. Henry, who was drunk, tried to convince me by a series of incoherent quotations, that Shakespeare was a communist. As my knowledge of Shakespeare was restricted to "A horse, a horse, my kingdom for a horse", I was not in a position to argue. Bidding Henry a brisk goodnight, I left him. I had got to the pavement when Henry from the top of the bus, declaiming "Once more into the breach", fell headlong down the stairs and split his skull on the kerb.

Dear Henry, I could have killed him! But at least he had the sense to crack his head open near Charing Cross Hospital which was then in the Strand. With blood streaming down his face, he was escorted there by two policemen. I waited until assured he would not only survive but be allowed out that night, then I went home to have a flaming row with Mother.

She was feeling down, the general outlook was lousy and the only anodyne she knew was alcohol. We were getting back to the old routine. For weeks I had been nagging, pleading, bullying, threatening to cut my share of the housekeeping. She in turn called me a stuck up, ungrateful bitch, Lady Muck with my fine clothes and fancy men, begrudging her the only pleasure in her life, a quiet drink with her friends. And now, by a stupid oversight on my part, she had found my savings book.

For years I had been saving small amounts from my pay and the balance now stood at forty pounds. When I was a child, I spake as a child, I understood as a child and one thing I had learned as a child and as a woman, although charity is a virtue, it is difficult to be either charitable or virtuous without money. That savings book Mother was brandishing under my nose may not have been the passport to paradise, but it was a small step on the way to self-respect and independence.

"Deceit, that's what it is! After all I've done for you. I suppose you earned that lot lying on your back!"

For the first and only time in my life I hit her. Hard. She fell back on the bed, rubbing her cheek in disbelief.

"To strike your own mother! Just wait until everyone hears about this!"

"There's plenty more where that one came from," I said.

It wasn't until that moment that my growing disenchantment with, and my estrangement from, the other families crystallized into a new awareness. Once again I was the odd one out. Almost all of my school mates had followed their parents' example and spent their free time in the pubs. Apart from Tom, Ivy and the Hutchings, I hardly passed the time of day with anyone.

"You can tell them something else, I'm getting out of this rotten place with or without you."

We were still quarrelling when Bill came home.

"Oh lor, oh lor," was all he could say when Mother almost triumphantly showed him the purple mark on her cheek.

"Striking your own mother! I've a good mind to have her done for assault!"

But she didn't report me and there was no need to tell the neighbours — that long-eared lot knew already. One consequence of all this was an unexpected understanding and alliance with Bill. We still hated each other, but we had a greater hatred in common, the tenements.

Resolution is one thing, execution another. I did not want to leave Hudsons, only the tenements. Bill wanted the country-side. Mother was going to see us both in hell before either of us got what we wanted.

114

The problem in London, as elsewhere, was too many people with too few houses to rent. Then some bright spark at County Hall came up with a solution — dump the poor, deserving and undeserving alike into a place in Essex called Dagenham. The site chosen was only twelve miles from Covent Garden and they started building homes fit for heroes to live in among the fields in 1921.

But all the stories were of mud and muddle and the ungrateful heroes, sick of mud and muddle, said, "Sod Dagenham." Gradually over the years the stories changed. Roads had been built, drainage laid and solidly built cottage-style houses had their own gardens. Rents were low and prospects of employment were good, particularly at Fords.

I had spent weeks in house hunting. Mother had toasted my every failure with an ostentatious tot of whisky.

"Here's mud in your eye," she would say in high good humour.

When Bill suggested Dagenham, which I had not even considered, Mother couldn't wait to share the joke with her cronies at the pub. That made up my mind, even if it meant giving up Hudsons. Dagenham it had to be. However, Mother was the legal tenant and without her agreement we could not get a transfer, and she was immovable.

The in 1934 Ramsay Macdonald or Baldwin made Hore-Belisha transport minister. If any man deserved a safe crossing to the other side that man was Hore-Belisha.

Oh cherubim and seraphim, loud hosannas of him sing, Belisha of the flashing beacon! And those studs between the lights, what an inspiration! In March 1935 Mother slipped on one and broke her ankle.

CHAPTER
FIVE

Dagenham and Other Diversions

Although I am making a joke of it now, at the time my main emotions were of guilt and anxiety that somehow I was responsible. Bill went into his usual trance of hear no evil, see no evil and do bugger all.

At Charing Cross Hospital they assured me that, despite a bad Potts fracture, Mother was in a good shape and swearing well. When she announced to the ward, "At last, here's my selfish bitch of a daughter," I threatened to break her other leg. After five days, no ambulance being available, I had to get her home for six weeks' complete bed rest.

Tom suggested using a coster's barrow. It might well have been easier, for it took all of Tom's massive strength to get her into a taxi and two men to get her out of it. Mother's figure was no longer trim but grim, not round but rectangular. It took three men, resting on every landing to lift, push and pull her up the five flights of stairs.

We solved the problem of keeping the foot upright by clamping it each side with flat-irons. With Ivy and Mrs

Hutchings's help at home and Jessie's help at work I survived the daily ritual of abuse and bedpan. Without Mother's wages I had to budget to the last farthing. I forced Bill to scrub and clean with the threat of "no work, no food". I rationed Mother to a half pint of beer a day. "Oh, you're hard," she would groan, "You're so hard it's unnatural." At the end of six weeks I was exhausted, but I was in charge.

Even with her ankle out of plaster Mother was confined to the tenement and her pals from the pub soon got fed up with climbing the stairs. She fumed and fretted to no avail; I kept a ruthless control of the budget. The start of the Civil War in Spain in July 1936 coincided with Mother's capitulation over the move to Dagenham.

My victory cost me dear. Without my money we could not have moved. And this is a point that planners overlooked, some people were simply too poor to move to Dagenham. This is why in 1936 there were still plenty of houses to choose from. They were all more or less alike, the trick was to get as near to shops and transport as possible.

Early in August I took my annual holiday. On the first Monday luck was with me all the way. On the Ilford section of the Becontree Estate, a four-roomed house had just become vacant because of rent arrears. It was twenty minutes walk from either Chadwell Heath or Goodmayes stations. Shops and the bus route to Ilford were less than two minutes away. I put down a deposit at once. On the Tuesday I took Mother and Bill to view. Although Mother complained bitterly all the way she was mollified by a drink at the *Royal Oak* which was, alas, also only two minutes walk from the house.

Within six weeks we had moved. Complaints about the Becontree Estate have multiplied over the years. There are those who regard it as an abomination, a blot on the landscape, but to me in 1936 it offered the promise of a much better life, a promise that was largely fulfilled, and this I have never forgotten.

To start with, the house had room for a garden front and back. Inside, although all the woodwork — floors, doors, window frames — were treated with creosote and the walls distempered an insipid shade of green, it was clean and free of bugs. In the living room the combination fire and oven was a little beauty and we had a gas cooker in the kitchen. The other three rooms had fire-places and, bliss itself, we had a separate bathroom. The hot water for the bath had to be pumped up by hand from the kitchen boiler, but this was no problem. There was a good sized larder and a separate coal cupboard. Our few sticks of furniture looked lost in so much space! At the back of the house was the church and vicarage of St Thomas's and, would you believe, tennis courts!

Bill and I got jobs immediately and with Mother's ten shillings a week old age pension we were financially viable from the start, although my savings book looked a bit sick. By financially viable I mean that we had enough to pay the rent and rates, the coal and gas bills, and to have an adequate diet.

My first job as a shop assistant was boring and badly paid, but within a month I was granted an interview for the position of manageress at Lush & Cook, dyers and cleaners in Green Lane, Dagenham. At the interview in Hackney I was complimented on my appearance, business aptitude and common sense. It was implied that the other interviewees were dead ducks. Within a fortnight I was on my way to a training school in Sussex with a month's pay in my pocket. Each entrant had to achieve a pass rate of eighty-five per cent before their employment was confirmed. My years at Hudsons paid off, I passed with one hundred per cent.

It was the start of a good time; business prospered and I prospered with it. In a month I was employing a full-time assistant as well as the errand boy. I was sent on several day courses at various factories to learn the latest techniques of dyeing and cleaning. I still knew nothing of Art, Literature or Politics and cared even less. My savings book was the only book that mattered and that made delightful bedtime reading.

Mother, a partly reformed character, stayed at home to do the cooking and cleaning and quarrel with the neighbours. Bill bought himself a bike, kept pigeons and rabbits and became knowledgeable about growing vegetables. On summer days there were still country lanes to explore and blackberries to pick. The one sad note was that Tom, Ivy and Jessie became like strangers and finally I stopped seeing them.

I still won prizes at whist drives and occasionally took a hand at the mating game at which I won no prizes at all. One affair with a fitter at Fords ran for about two years before he finally gave up. Other men came and went. If they were reasonably neat, clean and wanted to pay for my ticket to the cinema, music hall or whatever, that was fine. I made it clear from the start my knickers stayed on, with the result that I usually paid for my own ticket at the cinema, music hall or whatever.

On my free afternoons I used to meet up with the girls from the shops at Goodmayes, Ilford and Poplar to window-shop in the West End, have a meal and go to the theatre or cinema. I remember with affection the companionship, the wisecracking and the laughter. We had grand times.

At the beginning of 1939 I was sitting pretty. I was twenty-eight, well-paid, well-clothed, well-fed. Smart young men with briefcases came from Head Office to pay me compliments and hint at promotion.

By the end of the year, these same young men were volunteering for service in the armed forces. Henry's gloomy prognostications had at last come true: we were at war with Germany.

When the air raid siren sounded on that Sunday morning in September I was shocked, not by the warning itself, but by Mother's reaction to it. She, who had never shown fear before, was afraid. She was more than frightened, she was panic stricken. She had vivid memories of Liverpool Street Station being bombed in 1917. And now she wanted to run, she did not know where, just run. She took down the pictures of my father in his colour-sergeant's uniform and, cradling it in her arms as if it were a baby, ran to the door. Bill and

I managed to stop her and I, a bit shaken myself, went to the *Royal Oak* for a bottle of whisky. The whisky, I emphasized, was only to be used in an emergency. I don't know how many emergencies there were to a bottle, but by the time the phoney war was over and the Battle of Britain had begun, Mother was getting through a bottle every two or three weeks.

After Friday, 16 August 1940, Mother's consumption of whisky was not my primary concern. The Battle of Britain, the evacuation of children, the gas masks, the Anderson shelters, the blackout, the food rationing, the black market, have all been told with many variations in many books. I propose instead to tell the tale of the Battle of Ethel's Leg.

On Monday, 12 August I began a week's holiday. On the Thursday I took Mother and an aunt to see *Dear Octopus* at the Adelphi. After the show I went to stay with my aunt at New Malden, Surrey. Her house was a typical semi-detached on a tree lined estate. We spent the Friday morning in Kingston-on-Thames, had lunch, then laden with shopping caught the bus back to New Malden. It was a long walk from the bus stop. The streets were deserted. The afternoon turned hot and humid. The grass verges were parched, the leaves on the trees dusty, waiting for rain.

We were nearly home when the siren sounded. An air-raid warden, trying to put on his helmet and mount his bicycle at the same time, called out: "Take cover! Take cover!" We plodded on, sweating but unperturbed. Within seconds, it seemed, the sky was full of planes and bombs were bucketing down. The warden somersaulted from his cycle. The trees flared like torches, houses crumpled and fell. Shrapnel sliced through the air, then I was blown to the ground. I was able to turn my head and saw my aunt naked from the waist down stumbling to where her house had been. I tried to move but could not. Blood was pouring from both my legs, with the bone sticking out at an odd angle from the right one. God, Mother will be furious, I thought and laying my head back on my arms, I waited to die.

I was aware of people being dragged from houses and laid beside me. An empty drop-sided truck bounced its way around the craters. A dozen or more of us were loaded on like sides of beef, our blood mixing on the steel floor. I remained conscious during that terrible ride, but two women died. At Kingston County Hospital they decided to amputate my right leg. By this time I felt so rotten I didn't care, but I stubbornly refused to give the police my mother's name and address as next-of-kin.

The hospital was now swamped with casualties and there was no longer time to amputate that night. They took out what shrapnel they could, stitched up the wounds and packed my right leg in a spica plaster.

The next day I thought I was hallucinating, looking at myself standing by my bed. It was my aunt wearing my clothes! My suitcase had been blown intact into the road and my clothes were the only ones to survive the fire. During the weeks I was at Kingston, one of the wounds developed gas gangrene. They opened it up to find a piece of shrapnel three inches in diameter resting against the left femur which luckily remained intact. Not so the right one which was shattered. The official record, which I have seen, reads "comminuted fracture right leg and multiple wounds to left leg".

My right leg remained encased in the spica plaster, reaching from my foot to just under my armpits, with spaces for my toes, anus and vagina. The plaster became soaked in blood and stank the ward out. For the sake of other patients I was pushed out onto the balcony and began to know the meaning of fear. It was bad enough in the ward, the crump of bombs, the thud of the big guns, but out there alone, unable to move, the odd one out again, I was terrified.

On 12 September many of us were transferred to Botley's Park War Hospital, Chertsey, Surrey. We went in converted Green Line coaches, twenty stretchers to each coach. It was another hellish ride over badly damaged roads. On arrival we were laid out on the floor of a large hall, our names written on our foreheads with a colour to indicate the severity of injury. The hospital was made up of villas and each was full of casualties with only orange boxes separating the beds. The operating theatre was an emergency job with a corrugated roof. My first operation was a primitive one. Two nurses turned me over while a third poured surgical spirit straight from the bottle on to the open sores caused by the plaster cast.

At this time St Thomas's Hospital in Lambeth had been bombed out of action. Lambeth's tragic loss was our gain. The entire staff and what equipment could be salvaged came to Botley's and a proper orthopaedic ward was set up.

The two surgeons in charge of the ward were Mr Young and Mr Burns. They, with the help of those incomparable St Thomas's nurses, performed miracles. I believe three-quarters of the women patients and nurses were in love with Mr Young. He was pure Hollywood, tall, handsome, fair haired, blue eyed and had strong wonderfully shaped hands. I thought just my bloody luck to meet the one man I'd open my legs for and he's going to chop one off!

When they cut the plaster away, they found, along with a lot of maggots, that the leg was in the wrong position. X-rays were taken and the leg put in plaster again. Each time they did this I was under anaesthetic and each time I was sick for about three days afterwards.

At the end of October Mr Young told me that although he could amputate my leg with a pair of scissors as it was only held together by the main artery and some muscle, he wanted to save it. The fight for Ethel's leg was on. The pieces of bone were like a jigsaw. Each time I went to the operating theatre Mr Young would juggle a few more pieces back into place. The wound was then packed in a thick dressing soaked in acriflavine and a new spica plaster put back on.

Although we were twenty miles away we could still hear the raids on London, and in November when the devastating night bombing began we could see the red glow of London burning. As we were all Londoners in our ward there developed a rare sense of comradeship, sharing our few parcels and even fewer visitors. When not being sick, we were nearly always hungry. You needed to be hungry to eat the food anyway, it was awful.

Mary, a drug addict, who had been picked up in Hyde Park with both her legs broken and severe injuries to the body, had fits of screaming rage. When not sedated by Paraldehyde she was both lucid and witty. Hearing us moaning about the food she used to say, "Hold on, gels," and then take us through an imaginary banquet course after course, each with a different wine, a fantastic feast served on the finest Chinese porcelain by Nubian slaves.

"How's that, gels? You must feel better after that! But no nipping off with the Nubians, they're all mine! You can have the ambassadors and the diplomats if you like!"

It was unfortunate that my wound bled a lot and stunk to high heaven between operations. This also made some of the patients feel sick, although I had a sulphur candle burning on my locker day and night. But when the stench became too bad my bed was pushed out onto the verandah. Miss Odd One Out again. When the planes came growling overhead I would cover my head with the sheet and bite on my pillow. The nurses quickly understood my fears and some days I was in and out of the ward like a jack-in-the-box.

In December Mr Young fitted a few more fragments of my femur together. When I came round from the anaesthetic I could hear Joan weeping in the next bed as her arm was being dressed. Only two months married, Joan had lost an arm, her husband, father, mother, sisters and brothers all in one raid. I croaked out some sort of greeting and she pleaded the curtain be drawn back so I could reassure her that her wound was really healing. She could not bear to look at it for herself.

This became a daily ritual. At first it took all my small reserve of will-power to look at that raw stump, but that small act on my part helped to forge a deep bond between the nurses, Joan and myself.

The day sister was very beautiful, tall, slender, incredibly kind. Each night before going off duty she would kneel before the open fire in the centre of the ward, say a short prayer and wish us good night before switching off the lights. But on Christmas Eve her prayer gave us little comfort. I thought of the morrow, Christmas Day. The day for family reunion and rejoicing. From the beds around me came the cries of those who would never see their families again. Their misery increased my own sense of desolation and I made up my mind to have my leg off and be done with it. I gazed into the orange flames of the fire and relived again that day in August, the trees exploding into flame, my aunt stumbling half-naked to a house in ruins, and the waiting to die. Literally half-drugged, I felt drawn into an unreal world of flame and shadow, of delirium and delusion.

I heard as in a dream the choir of St Clement Danes. But others seemed to hear it too. Heads were turning and eyes strained to see beyond the shadows. The sweet sound came nearer. The door at the end of the ward opened and into the half light came forty or more nurses with their dark capes thrown back to show the red linings.

Some nurses carried lanterns, others played violins and they all sang like angels. They moved through the ward and then onto the next villa, and the next. I listened to those last lingering notes and wept with sorrow and with joy. I pretended to be asleep when the night sister quietly laid a small parcel beside each bed.

On Christmas morning we were like excited children opening our parcels. Each had a new face cloth and a bar of good soap, or a cloth with a new toothbrush, all precious items. After being washed and dressings renewed, we each had a real egg for breakfast. All the nurses came on duty joking, laughing, teasing and soon the whole ward began to respond. And the dinner!

Amid cheers and applause, and wearing their surgeon's coats but with high chef's hats, Mr Young and Mr Burns wheeled in the trolley with a huge roast turkey and mounds of vegetables. They took turns at carving.

"After you, Mr Burns."

"After you, Mr Young."

"You've been practising, Mr Burns."

"Indeed, and you're no amateur, Mr Young."

And the double act went on, with nurses hurrying round with plates piled high. Three enormous puddings alight with brandy came after with jugs and jugs of custard. What a gorgeous Christmas! I slept well that night dreaming of Mr Young, and he wasn't playing Santa Claus!

New Year's Day 1941 was not so pleasant. I had a fever and there were admitted to the ward the four Ballard sisters and the Gresham twins. All had suffered the most dreadful injuries, broken arms and legs, burns and shrapnel wounds to their bodies and head. A small room usually kept for equipment was cleared out spacially for them. The Ballard sisters had had a dairy and grocery business in Golders Green. The shop was gutted and their parents killed. The youngest was fifteen and the oldest twenty-three. The Gresham twins from Kensington were nineteen and had been fashion models, but wouldn't be again. Mr Young and Mr Burns and the nurses worked round the clock to save them and somehow they did.

Mrs Gale was a trump at times like this. She was about fifty, very formal and correct at first, obviously a beauty in her time. She owned, or had owned, a private laundry in Chelsea which had been bombed out. Both of her legs and one arm had been broken and she had wounds to her head. Her husband and daughter had luckily survived with only superficial injuries. It was weeks before Mrs Gale accepted us for the motley crew we were and we were allowed to call her Mum. She was great and insisted that her husband bought as much on the black market as he and her daughter could carry and then shared the booty among the rest of us. Mum was cheerful, charming and generous and we remained friends for years.

On 24 January, 1941 I insisted that if my leg was not taken off, I would have the next operation without anaesthetic.

"You are either very brave or very stupid, Ethel," said Mr Young. I was stupid. They strapped me to a sort of scaffolding so that they could work under as well as round me. The anaesthetist, holding my hand, said, "Just say the word, Ethel, and I'll put you out." The operation lasted over three hours, but the pain made a mockery of time. I was in a nightmare ministered to by passing ghosts. When I returned to the ward for a cup of tea, I was the centre of attention. I tried to play the part of the heroine, but my courage was shot to hell. I could never go through that ordeal again.

I recovered from another fever in time to be wheeled in a basket-bed arrangement to see an ENSA concert. The small theatre, built before the war, was downhill in the hospital grounds. The night was very cold and black. We were made comfortable, then the nurses hurried back to their work in the wards. We were singing *Bless them all* when the sirens wailed. Appeals were made for helpers to push the wheelchair cases. A burly sergeant seized my bed as if it were a child's pram and we set off up the hill. As the first bombs fell, the sergeant dived for cover and my bed ran backwards into the kerb. The sergeant stumbled to his feet and disappeared.

"For God's sake don't leave me here!" I called after him, but he was gone. I was left alone in my now familiar nightmare of flares and incendiaries, the frantic searchlights, the bomb bursts and the thump, thump,

thump of the guns. When the nurses found me I was numb with cold and terror. Even now whenever I hear an aircraft flying low my gut reaction is for my stomach muscles to tighten into a knot and the words "Let is be one of ours" come unbidden to mind.

Soon after this I was up on crutches and could manage a smart hundred yards sprint to the mortuary and back. Then I could chat up some of the survivors from Dunkirk. Among them was Pierre, a small Frenchman who made a declaration of undying love and chased me round and round a table in an otherwise deserted canteen. As we were both on crutches and encased in plaster, his passion had little prospect of being consummated. But you can never tell with the French, they have a reputation for ingenuity in such matters.

On 24 March they injected gas into the wound to lift the scar and so enable them to cut the unwanted lesions preventing normal manipulation by weight and pulley. A gutter plaster, to the groin only, allowed easier access to the wound and I could move around with walking sticks. Mr Young told me that it was a very interesting operation and I said something rude. He roared with laughter and said:

"That's my girl."

"Any time, Mr Young, any time," I replied.

As he and his highly amused entourage departed, the sister said: "You're a brazen hussy and you're way behind in the queue anyway." For months my knee was manipulated each day for an hour.

In June Mother was reported to be dying and I was so distraught that arrangements were considered for sending me home for a few days. I should have known Mother better. She was suffering from an acute attack of shingles, not cessation of breath. Nevertheless, I was oppressed by the old feeling of guilt. Somehow, however obscurely, I was responsible for her illness and should be at home to nurse her. Mr Young was not impressed.

"You are not in a position to nurse anyone, Ethel. If you're feeling so energetic, we'll give that leg more work to do."

The manipulations increased and I received full marks for effort. But my efforts and those of the therapist, a golden girl called Helen, were not enough. In January 1942 the knee was forcibly manipulated while I was under anaesthetic.

On 5 February they tried again and on 26 February yet again. But this time the scar burst open and apparently there was blood everywhere. Happily a proposal to graft tissue from my backside to cover the wound was rejected. According to Ivy all those years ago, my legs and my bum were my best assets in the mating game and, with my legs shot to blazes, I was now, as it were, down to base.

I was back on the operating table on 19 and 28 May and both times the scar held up. A few days later I was helped out of bed and fully dressed. Mr Young, Mr Burns and Helen came into the ward and stood some distance from me.

"Stand up, Ethel." I stood up.

"Walk over here." I looked around for my sticks.

"No sticks! Walk!" So urgent, so compelling was Mr Young's voice that, like a child with arms outstretched, I took my first precarious unaided steps. I lurched rather than walked for one leg was shorter than the other.

"You've done it, Ethel, you've done it," he said triumphantly.

For a moment he held me and I thought: "Christ, for that I'd have climbed bloody Everest!"

Mr Young rejected all talk of surgical shoes.

"Why advertise the fact that you're a cripple."

He taught me to walk almost normally by tilting my pelvis.

Before I left Botleys I achieved another ambition. For one day only I was the heroine in the centre of the stage taking my bow before a full house of doctors and physiotherapists. They had come from all over the country. My X-rays were blown up in size, projected on a screen and Mr Young went through my rehabilitation step by step.

At the end, to tremendous applause he bowed to me, I curtsied to him and hand in hand we walked from the stage. We had a splendid dinner, after which I was bombarded with questions and congratulations.

When I was asked "What are you going to do now?" I had no idea. I could not stay at the hospital nor did I want to, but where to go? I tried to disguise my increasing anxiety but Mr Young knew me too well.

"It would be unwise to go back to the stress of Dagenham. The thing is, can you cook?"

"Of course I can cook."

"Right, I'll introduce you to Sarah Quigley one of our V.A.Ds. She's taking lessons on how to boil an egg."

Mrs Quigley was about thirty, tall, good long legs, big teeth, very county; someone whose world had come temporarily unstuck for lack of a cook-housekeeper. Whatever her ineptitude as a cook she was brisk and efficient as a potential employer. She could offer what I wanted, I could offer what she needed, why not give it a try?

"Come along and look at the house and have a chat with Nanny."

I remember how peaceful the golden fields looked in the July sunshine as we drove along the quiet country roads. The house was foursquare, large, old and ugly. Nanny was small, old and a charmer. A white-haired, bright-eyed pixie, she sat in an enormous chair with her feet curled under her and told me the story of the Quigleys.

They were, it seemed, paragons of employers for whom she had first worked as a tweenie. Now she had her own suite of drawing room, bedroom and bathroom. Her sole responsibility was two shy boys of three and five. Mr Quigley, whom she had nursed as a baby, was something hush-hush in the MOD who supplied him with an army batman called John who acted as butler. Two women and two gardeners came in from the nearby village to do the housework and gardens. My job would be to cook and co-ordinate.

"Ethel, my dear, it's pushover," said Nanny.

John, who came in with a tray of tea agreed with her. He then showed me to my room. What a room! It was enormous, thickly carpeted, with a splendid double bed, two large wardrobes, a dressing table, an armchair and a bathroom and toilet!

But it was the kitchen that really threw me. One half was a sitting room with an open fire, comfortable chairs and a table. The working half had two large ovens, one gas, one electric. There were rows and rows of gleaming pots and pans, some enamel, some copper, some steel and enough cutlery to carve your way through a troop of cavalry. A huge refrigerator had plenty of milk, butter, eggs, cheese, fish and meat. A cupboard was crammed with tins and packets of groceries. Yet another cupboard held china and glassware.

On the north wall was a store room with shelving for fruit and vegetables and hooks for hanging game and poultry. Most of this came up from the Quigley estate in Hampshire. To cap it all, John said:

"Here are two telephone numbers. This is for the car service and this one for the provision merchant. Should you need either, charge everything to the Quigley account."

In my drab old clothes I felt I had landed the part of Cinders at last.

"When you're ready," said John, "Mrs Quigley will see you in the library."

I sat down to think it out. John made another pot of tea and I ate my way through a plate of chicken and ham sandwiches. I was no longer bothered about

135

whether I could do the job but such extravagance in war time seemed almost indecent. John had no doubts.

"This is a different world, Ethel. We didn't make the rules. Of course it isn't fair. It never was and never will be."

I should have liked to wipe the expectant smile from Mrs Quigley's face but she didn't bat an eyelid when I made one of my conditions of employment a full day free each week with the use of the car service to take one or two of the patients from Botleys into Woking.

"Fine," she said, "Mr Quigley will be in, so we'll have dinner at seven-thirty. I'll leave everything entirely to you."

I gave them soup, fish, egg custard, cheese and biscuits. John made the coffee. No problem, no big deal either. I was astonished when they came into the kitchen to congratulate me. Mr Quigley was handsome in dinner jacket and bow tie, Mrs Quigley elegant in a long black gown. They asked me to celebrate my first evening with a glass of wine.

When I went upstairs I soaked for a long time in the bath. Then I looked at my skinny body in the full length mirror. No tits, bashed up legs, even the tops of my thighs and bum had shrivelled.

"Oh what the hell!" I thought, and clambering into my lovely bed, fell instantly asleep.

I was woken at seven o'clock by a tap on the door and in walked John with a breakfast tray of coffee, a boiled egg, toast and marmalade, plus a newspaper! While he pulled the curtains, I demurely covered my non-existent breasts and decided to buy some new nightdresses.

Mr Quigley usually left home at seven o'clock and I would be up and ready with Madam's breakfast by eight-thirty.

The first day I went over the entire house with the two helpers. Ugly old place though it was on the outside, the inside was really luxurious with eight bedrooms, four of them with en suite bathrooms. Within a week I was organized.

There was a shelf of cookery books in the kitchen and I had a lot of fun working out more extravagant meals. With a soufflé for instance, I would make two and put one in each oven. One had to come out right!

Clothes were high on my list of priorities. Nanny gave me (ask no questions and you get told no lies) a dozen pairs of black silk stockings, three saucy nightdresses and some underwear. I had a full book of clothing coupons and back pay from the Ministry of Pensions, plus my pay from the Quigleys.

On my first day off I ordered the car, took a bag of sandwiches and cakes to the hospital and then carted Mrs Gale (Mum) to Woking. She could get around on crutches now and her hair was beginning to grow again. Her pleasure was so infectious that even the driver, a crabby old man, had to smile. She was going to buy a dozen hats; she ended up with two. I bought two severely classical dresses and a pair of good leather shoes. Mum generously let me have some of her coupons and I was able to get a good summer coat as well. It was a lovely day and she was such fun, I was sorry when it was over.

Each week I was able to take someone. Joan was emotional. Mary behaved so outrageously I was afraid we would get arrested. What with the food I took to the hospital and the carhire charges, these jaunts of mine must have cost the Quigleys a fortune. On top of that I was sending discreet parcels home. Mother's acknowledgements were usually admonishments.

"I hope you know what you are doing" and "Behave yourself."

I did not tell her about John and my breakfasts in bed. I was putting on weight which, according to the mirror and the gleam in John's bright eye, was ending up in the right places. Working so much together, casual encounters of breast and thigh were inevitable. I did not avoid them, neither did I deliberately invite them for he was years younger than I, and also engaged to a girl in Richmond. At times like this I thought of Jessie and sought blessed relief within myself.

When Nanny and the children came into the kitchen and found John and me hip to hip at the sink or bending over a cookery book her old eyes twinkled and she would give me a wicked wink. I used to poke out my tongue and create a diversion by making a fuss of William and Harold. Nanny was all love but she was old, tired easily, and the kids had no real fun. I had a bright idea.

Why should I not take them out one afternoon and give Nanny a break? Nanny and the children were all for it, but Madam was full of maternal alarm. I had planned to take them on a Green Line coach to the river at Chertsey. This simply would not do.

We finally set out by car with John as escort and to carry the cotton clothes and sandals (should it be hot) and woollen coats and wellington boots (should it be cold) and so on, and so on. What a bloody rigmarole!

Nevertheless we enjoyed ourselves, fed our sandwiches to the swans and ate ice cream cornets instead. We hired a boat and tried to catch minnows with a couple of cheap fishing nets. John had his arm around my waist several times on one pretext or another and I felt a buzz of sexual excitement.

I spoilt it a little when we decided to paddle. Taking off my stockings I unintentionally revealed my wound. When John saw it he said, "Christ" and put out a hand.

"Don't you dare touch it," I blazed at him.

With difficulty I controlled the turmoil I was in for the kids were going wild with pleasure, splashing each other and us. Because of my shortened leg and not wanting to be a spoilsport, I had to let John hold me while I dabbled my toes in the water. But from that moment on I intended to discourage any further close encounters.

Almost immediately on our return, however, we had an encounter of a different kind. Mr Quigley had invited Lord and Lady Blank to dinner the next evening. We had two plump chickens in store so I asked John to get them out, chop off their heads and help me to pluck them. Everything went fine until I started to take out the giblets. I shrieked and John said: "Bloody hell-fire!" as I drew out a handful of maggots.

I went to Nanny for advice but she was more interested in my affair with John.

"There is no affair and you're a naughty old lady. What am I going to do with these bloody maggots?"

"Cook 'em," she said, "no one will notice."

But good old trooper that she was, she came down and helped John and I wash and rewash the chickens. John burnt the giblets in the garden. When we gave the insides a final rinse with whisky it was past midnight.

As soon as John came in with my breakfast tray, I sat up to ask: "How are the chickens?"

"Fine, as fresh as the morning dew."

He was splendid that day, helping me to prepare various sauces and vegetables, the different combinations of sweets and fresh fruit salad. Enough food went out of that kitchen that evening to feed a dozen families in Covent Garden or a ward at Botleys. When John came in for the coffee he was fuming.

"That silly old bugger reckons no-one in England knows how to make coffee. He wants it really black."

"Bung a piece of coal in the percolator," I suggested, and John did just that. I went weak at the knees. Maggots in the chickens and coal in the coffee! I sat down and waited for the balloon to go up. Nothing happened. I opened the kitchen door but all I could hear was the steady boom — boom — boom of Lord Blank's voice.

When John came out of the dining room at nine-thirty he was closely followed by the Quigleys and the Blanks. Lord Blank was massive, purple faced and very much in charge. Lady Blank was very, very attractive, dark as a gypsy in a simple white gown. They were effusive with their compliments, the meal was splendid and they all gave me a hug and a kiss. Lord Blank, putting a huge hand on John's shoulder said:

"That was the best coffee I've had for years."

When they left, I forgot my good intentions and fell laughing and kissing into John's arms. We began to kiss for real, but as soon as his hand went below my waist I automatically went into reverse. It was just as well, Mrs Quigley came in a moment later to find us both at the sink. Although she could not thank us enough, she made no attempt to help with the washing-up.

A few days later Nanny and the children left to stay for a while in Hampshire. I missed them very much. I was becoming increasingly fond of John which was a complication, but I felt a growing unease when he wasn't there, on leave to Richmond for example. When I walked alone in the garden, although there were no planes in the sky, I felt vulnerable and used to hurry breathlessly back to the house.

Later in October Mr and Mrs Quigley decided to join the children for the weekend. John and I spent the Saturday pleasantly together and sat down amiably enough to an evening meal of fresh salmon, baked apples and cream. He opened a bottle of Sauterne and urged me to drink up and be happy. He had port with his biscuits and cheese and then began on the brandy.

As I started to clear the table he began on me. Almost sadly I pushed him away but, sure enough, out popped his pride and joy. I reached down, grabbed a handful and turned the whole lot smartly in a clockwise direction. He gave a deep groan, fell across the sink and was promptly sick.

I finished clearing the table and washing up while he lay moaning and cursing on the floor. It occurred to me that most swearing was unoriginal and repetitive. As I stepped over him I said:

"You know what you remind me of?"

I apparently was a prick teaser, a cow and a bitch.

"And you," I said, "are like the wind in a sheep's belly — you make a lot of noise and you stink!"

Stink he certainly did of vomit and drink. I helped him to his feet. Somehow I got him to his room, undressed him, washed him down avoiding the painful parts, and then bundled him naked into bed. Before getting into my own bath, I looked at myself in the mirror. I though of John's body and wondered what would have happened had he not been drunk.

On Sunday there was no breakfast in bed. I dressed and went along to John's room. He looked a wreck.

"How are you, John?"

"My balls hurt and I've got a rotten headache," he said sullenly.

"Hard luck! I'll give you half an hour to shave and dress, then I'll start cooking breakfast."

He looked clean but thoroughly miserable when he came down, but it is amazing what eggs, bacon, toast and coffee can do.

"John, I'm thinking of packing this lot in and if I do, I should like us to part friends."

Alarmed he said, "You'll not tell the Quigleys about me?"

"Of course not, you fool."

I went on to explain that I hated drink and at thirty-one I was still a virgin. We then got down to a long heart-to-heart about sex. Not only was he a virgin as well, but his girlfriend was a bigger prude than I was.

"I've seen more of your tits than I ever have of hers," he said.

"You never did."

"I did! Especially that weekend when the Blanks were here!" He added wistfully: "You've got lovely nipples, Ethel, like ripe raspberries."

"Really! Would you like them with or without cream, Sir?" I should not have said that.

On my next day off I explained to Mum the fix I was in. I was deeply grateful to the Quigleys, but with Nanny still away, John was becoming more persistent, and the cold November wind cutting across the bleak countryside was beginning to get on my nerves.

I had already met Mrs Field, Mum's sister, who lived in Baldock, Hertfordshire, with their mother. We phoned from Woking there and then and she agreed to have me. The problem of transport was solved, Mum's husband would take me by car.

Next I had to face Mrs Quigley, but she made it easy for me.

"Oh Ethel" she called out in her county voice as she came down from the library. "We shall all be going to Hampshire for Christmas, including you and John. Will you make the arrangements?"

I told her I would not be there for Christmas; I was leaving for good at the beginning of December.

She sat down on the stairs and wept in sheer vexation.

"Oh Ethel, how could you? How could you!" Then vindictively: "I suppose you want more money, is that it? How much *do* you want?"

If she had used the argument that they had grown fond of me or Nanny and the children were looking forward to seeing me, it might well have changed my mind.

"Try thirty pieces of silver," I retorted and banged the kitchen door behind me. I was so distressed that when John tried to comfort me I boxed his ear and burst into tears. The more I thought about it, the more foolish seemed my decision. I sat in my cosy kitchen with the logs blazing in the fireplace and looked around the shelves at the jams, preserves and chutneys that I had made and wished I could find an excuse to retract my notice.

When the time came to leave, Mrs Quigley refused to see me and my parting with John was an anti-climax. We shook hands and I promised to write, but never did. It was pouring with rain and my face was quite wet as I got into Mr Gale's big old car and we headed for Baldock.

CHAPTER SIX

Baldock and Letchworth

Baldock was a prosperous country town with a pleasant market square, a row of "picture book" alms houses complete with boxes and tubs of flowers in summer. St Mary's church, the centre about which the town had grown, did not excite the reverence I felt for St Clement Danes, but I felt comfortable there. There was a brewery and, despite my aversion to alcohol, I was convinced that the smell of fermenting hops was good for me. It was an environment and an atmosphere entirely new to me and I liked it.

Mrs Field, Trixie, was plump, fifty, unflappable except when she caught her mother, Tilly, smoking. Tilly was a mischievous seventy-year-old whose greatest pleasure was outwitting Trixie. They were both wonderfully kind and supportive to me, accepting me at once as "family". But it was at Baldock I went through some of the worst periods of my life, at times breaking down completely.

I had not known beforehand that around Baldock were airfields from which the heavy American bombers known as Flying Fortresses made regular raids on Germany. They came over Baldock in waves of only six or seven, but there was no escaping the grinding, growling menace of their engines. This noise seemed to split me apart and crush me into the ground at one and the same time.

Trixie was convinced, and at first convinced me, that I could adapt to the knowledge that these planes were not foes but friends and be able to face each day without fear. In the meantime I had to earn a living.

Only ten minutes walk away was the Kayser Bondor stocking factory where several of Trixie's neighbours worked. I was able to join them quite naturally when I started work there. With dozens of other women I checked stockings for flaws as they came off the machines. Payment was by result; I did not earn much. I had neither the manual dexterity nor the temperament for the job.

Within a month I began to lose the sense of physical well-being acquired at the Quigleys. Worse still was my loss of self-confidence. Within another month I was emotionally and physically exhausted.

In order to survive economically, if you are sick, you need a medical certificate. To get a medical certificate you must go to a doctor. You must use the system and for good or ill you become locked into the system. I went to a doctor and he sent me to a psychiatrist. The battle of Ethel's mind was on, compared to which the battle for Ethel's leg was a pushover.

There was no gifted Mr Young to come to the rescue this time. Compared to him the doctors I encountered were clumsy amateur mechanics. In an attempt to be fair I'll accept that a fractured femur may be easier to mend than a fractured mind. Finally, surprise, surprise, my fear, my terror was brilliantly diagnosed as "anxiety neurosis". My situation was complicated by the need to attend frequent examinations by Ministry Medical Officers.

Some of these were not only incompetent bastards, but brutal, incompetent bastards whose intention was to degrade and humiliate. The theory may have been to make me too ashamed to receive a pension. In practice they added to my anxiety, making me confused, depressed, wretched, but they also lit a tiny spark of anger which grew into a healthy flame.

I have never been able to rid myself totally of my "anxiety" that some unnamed terror might fall from the sky, but I did get rid of my fear of Ministry of Pensions Officials. I became in their words, "bitter", another masterly understatement. I hated their guts. But again, and this time I mean it, they are more pleasant these days, probably because they expect me to drop dead soon anyway.

Between November 1942 and November 1947 I had months of psychotherapy and psychological explanation and suggestions for readjustment. The reasons for my anxiety, my phobia, as it is called, were gone over again and again and again; the trauma of the orphanage, the injuries received at New Malden, the terrible night of the concert.

In 1945, perhaps 1946, one Dr Mannheim introduced a new variation on the theme, fear of sex. If nothing else it provided new interest to the otherwise routine question and answer exchanges. I admitted masturbating (did not everyone?) and at times of stress probably more so as a release from physical tension. We certainly went to town during these sessions, but I did not accept his basic premise. Fear of becoming pregnant yes, but not of sexual intercourse. I refused point blank to believe that sex had anything to do with my crippling anxiety or phobia. Some of our talks took place in the open air, strolling about the green at Hitchin. When I told him about my assault on poor John's private parts, the good Doctor gave an uncharacteristic high-pitched giggle. I bet more than one passer-by heard more than was good for them.

There was plenty of sexual activity going on in Baldock during the war. The Americans were for ever "chasing tail" as they quaintly called it and had plenty of money to pay for it in one way or another. They livened up the place no end with their drinking, fighting and fornication. One of their commanding officers was reputed to have said, "If they can't fuck, they won't fight," which made me wonder whether I was doing enough for the war effort.

All this time, when not attending hospital, I was still working at Kayser Bondor. I had quit the factory floor and had become a wages clerk, a job that fitted me like a glove. I enjoyed working out piece-time and overtime rates and the racing against the clock to get the pay packets made up in time.

I was faster even than Two Gun Dick. He had been one of the aircrew of a night-flying Lancaster, which had crashed on returning to England. As the sole survivor he had been invalided out. He was a very handsome young man, good at his job but always began to twitch as the tension built up. He used to twitch his eyebrows, his ears, his nose, his shoulders and his thumbs would go crack, crack, as he worked faster and faster. I dare not watch him, or I should have begun to twitch too, but I enjoyed the challenge of racing both him and the clock.

This challenge took place every Friday morning when we and two others from our office and four senior heads of other departments were locked in the "dungeon", a strong room. We had to check the money collected from the bank in Baldock and then make up the wages from the lists already prepared by the wages office. The dungeon was underground. It had no windows. We were locked in but I felt no fear at all. I used to look forward to it, the excitement, the triumph of beating the clock.

Over half the factory had been converted for the production of cathode ray tubes for radar equipment. To make extra space for that work, we were moved out to a temporary building known by us all as the "chicken run". The conditions in the chicken run were primitive with broken up cardboard boxes to cover the concrete floor, and the asbestos walls distempered a flaky white.

We had various dignitaries come to visit the factory, Stafford Cripps looking like an anorexic lamp post, I remember, but these people were normally shown only the production line and were carefully shepherded throughout their visit to a pre-arranged plan.

Queen Mary, bless her valiant heart, would have nothing to do with pre-arranged plans. With a wave of her umbrella she relegated her sycophantic escort to the rear and, with Princess Margaret in tow, made straight for the chicken run. We, watching from the windows, were sent back to our desks by the agitated chief clerk. As she swept in, the other clerks kept their heads bent over their work, but I was not going to miss a thing.

She was tall, erect, regal. At one glance she seemed to take in every dingy detail. Perhaps because I was the only one looking directly at her, and my admiration and affection so obvious, she came straight to me. Her face was stern and unsmiling, her questions direct and uncompromising. I felt quite, quite calm. I said my work was simple but enjoyable. She moved a piece of cardboard with the point of her umbrella.

"And this?" she asked, indicating in just two words the condition of the office.

One of the managers hurried forward eager to explain but was stopped in his tracks by her stony disregard.

"And this?" she asked again. I said it was a temporary arrangement.

"You have a canteen?"

"Yes."

"And the food?"

"Adequate but monotonous."

"I see. Adequate but monotonous," she repeated and I swear there was a flicker of amusement in those eyes.

I added gratuitously: "Kayser Bondor are very good employers."

"I'm pleased to hear it." And with a slight inclination of her head she was gone, her retinue falling over themselves to get out of her way. I was serenely indifferent to the chief clerk's angry strictures of what I should or should not have done. However, his objection that I was showing too much leg was unfortunately, on this occasion, only too true. My skirt was well above my knees. I'm sure that Queen Mary could not have approved.

Trixie frequently rebuked me for my lack of attention to such detail; Dr Mannheim saw it as affirming my ambivalent attitude towards sexual congress. As Trixie was my constant chaperone and guide to the social life of Baldock, I had to pay more attention to her than I did to Dr Mannheim. She even persuaded the choir mistress of St Mary's to let me join the choir, which was tough on the rest of the choir. After practice we used to nip into the pub next door, *The George*, just before closing time.

The George was a splendid pub with large open fireplaces blazing with logs on winter nights. Inevitably it was monopolized by American airmen knocking back whisky. I did not blame them for that. It was their continual propositioning and pawing I could not stand. On Saturday nights they held dances at one of their airfields and provided transport for the girls of Baldock to attend. On Monday mornings in the office there was a competition to see who had been given the most pairs of nylons, underwear, or boxes of candy. Not everyone took part in this, but I was surprised by the avarice of those who did. Their placid, pleasant country faces were sharp with greed, and gave some credence to the G.I.'s jibe at our servicemen:

"Your beer is dear, but your women are cheap enough."

I went only once to one of the dances, but I went by taxi with three other "doubtfuls". The idea was to provide each other with moral support. On being confronted by a six foot four inch slab of muscle, I thanked him for his suggestion but regretted that I had venereal disease. Now my knowledge of venereal disease was as scanty as my knowledge of Shakespeare, but when this handsome hero replied: "That's all right, sweetheart, I've got syphilis anyway," I got the hell out of there fast, leaving the other doubtfuls to their fate. Thank God the taxi was still waiting.

I have not felt the need to extend my knowledge of venereal disease but a German Jewess refugee shamed me into learning something of William Shakespeare.

I had been bemoaning the lack of a theatre in Baldock and was promptly challenged to do something about it by Mr Hancock, headmaster of the local school.

"Find ten other people interested in forming a drama class and I'll get the money to pay a teacher."

I found ten other people, but Mr Hancock was not letting me stop there. With Trixie for support I was sent to see Katie Steinfeld.

I have no idea how a penniless Jewish actress unable to speak English came to Baldock, but there she was living rent-free by courtesy of the De Beer family in a tiny room at the top of an old house facing the market square. She looked old, her skin yellowish, hair thin and straggly, her eyes without lustre.

As a child I had acquired a small skill in communicating as an unofficial guide to tourists in London. Katie watched impassively while Trixie and I strutted about the room miming actors and audience. When she finally understood she clapped her hands and those wonderful eyes came alive. We wanted to take her for a meal but she would have none of it. She insisted we went down to the kitchen in the basement where she made us cheese and potato cakes. Gone was the old lady. This was a quick, alert fifty-year old.

We went to see Mr Hancock and the crafty old devil spoke to her in fluent German. He had known about her from the De Beers, had known that she was an actress and that her husband and son were still caged in a concentration camp. What none of us had anticipated were her gifts as a teacher. The energy flowing from that body was incredible. She could slip out of the skin of one character into another, from a lithe young Prince Hal to a pot-bellied Falstaff by a change of voice and the shift of weight from her hips. All this in an old brown dress and without a trace of make-up.

I have seen St Joan played many times but never as Katie played it. Her body was a living flame with all the torment of not only the Jews but the whole human race writhing at the stake. At first she had to rely on Mr Hancock to translate her texts into German and her German into English. She quickly acquired a sufficient command of English to impose her complete authority over us. Her fiat was final.

I, feeling deserving of glory, was relegated to walk on parts, general dogsbody and prompt. I had to learn everyone's part, and some of Shakespeare's plays are unbelievably boring to read. If I were still able to go to the theatre and had the choice of *Romeo and Juliet* or *West Side Story*, it would be the latter every time.

"You are," Katie would say, "You are, what do you call it . . . a Philistine!"

Katie placed Baldock well and truly on the amateur drama map and the group went on to win several awards. Our *Children in Uniform* had rave reviews and our photographs were in the local papers. We were invited to Welwyn Garden City and received standing ovations there. I know the group continued for twenty-five years until Katie died and for all I know continues still.

It was Trixie and Trixie alone who deserves the credit for introducing Old Time Dancing to Baldock. It started in her dining room with an old gramophone and a few records. She taught me the dances partly to strengthen my leg, but I enjoyed it so much that a couple of engineers were roped in as partners. Others clamoured to join and within weeks we were hiring a hall, a six-piece band and making a small profit from the tickets. We were then able every three months or so to go to town, hiring the town hall, having special cards printed in the old style with small pencils attached by silken cords.

People came from villages for miles around, the gentlemen in evening suits and the ladies in long dresses. Happy the lady whose card was filled before the dancing began. Although half-serious skirmishes in the mating game added to the excitement of the Gay Gordons, the Minuets and Quadrilles, alcohol was forbidden so no-one made fools of themselves.

One of the engineers, a Yorkshireman, was a very accomplished dancer and he became my teacher and partner. We went to dances as far afield as Watford and even won prizes, only boxes of chocolates and that type of thing, but it was gratifying. He also stirred my loins quite a bit but not only was he happily married, his manners and his morals were as impeccable as his dancing. Life was good and agreeable.

During the day by skilful use of acquaintances and taxis, I was able to keep panic under control, although the fear of fear was always present. But there was no way I could evade the horrors that took their revenge at night and brought Trixie hurrying to my bed and cradle me in her arms like a mother with a child.

During this time I was sending long descriptive letters home and received the usual laconic replies. When I was able to make the journey with Trixie, Mother seemed genuinely pleased to see me although she never said as much. Once Tilly came with us and she and Mother had a high old time at the *Royal Oak*. Tilly and her husband, Trixie's father, had once owned a pub, so there was plenty to talk about. Tilly came home like a smoked kipper and Mother like a soused herring. They shared Mother's bed and we could hear them still laughing at two in the morning.

As a result of one of my bizarre misadventures in the mating game I took home to meet Mother a sad, sad man called Douglas. He was stationed temporarily at an Army Transit Camp north of Baldock. Our chaps were unable to compete with the free-spending Americans, but Trixie working in town got to know a few by name and invited them to the house for a cup of tea and a sing song. Among them was Douglas.

What followed was pathetic, so idiotic, so implausible, if it were not for the fact that I ended up in bed with Douglas, I would not tell the tale at all. He was tall, good looking, had plenty of money. His marriage had never been consummated and if I would marry him he would get a divorce.

This all happened within a few weeks, a brief romance with a few kisses and my libido barely warm, let alone on fire. What a crazy cocked-up affair! Well, not cocked up, more cocked down.

To start with we visited his married sisters and mother who lived in Dulwich. They were delighted with me and I was impressed with them. They were well off for a start and, let's face it, I was no spring chicken and, as Ivy had said, if the right one doesn't come along you have to make do with what's left over. So I took him to see Mother who took me into the kitchen and told me not to be a bloody fool. We then went to see his wife, a very sick lady who cared not a damn about the proposed divorce.

The house was well-built, spacious, detached and my brain started clocking up pounds, shillings and pence. I must have still been doing sums when he suggested that we spend the night together in London. The hotel was clean, the food good and the bedroom comfortable.

Douglas could not wait to get into action. I did my best to co-operate, but my vaginal muscles were more effective than a chastity belt. Douglas's erection, such as it was, could not sustain a prolonged assault. He and his erection collapsed together. At first he cried, then he became angry. All women were the same, common tarts after his money. Well, I had asked for that one I suppose.

He went on and on ranting and raving, swearing, crying, until I told him to put his nappies on and go to bed. He began to behave like a madman and I thought he would kill me. Fortunately I had put my clothes back on. I grabbed my bag and ran. My heart was pounding like a kettle drum. I asked the night porter to get me a taxi and I spent the rest of the night closeted with the station master while I waited for the first train to Baldock. I resolved never to be involved with men again, ever. I would save my money and die a virtuous old maid.

Trixie was not pleased with my affair with Douglas, but then neither was I. I had behaved like a fool and a mercenary fool into the bargain. Mannheim explained my behaviour in terms of need for security, but my self-respect had taken quite a blow. While continuing to enjoy the social life of Baldock my attitude towards men was short, sharp and matter of fact. It is said that women suffer from penis envy. I wonder how many men suffer from penis inadequacy?

On V.E. Night I did not behave with total propriety, but not many did. For weeks we had been preparing for peace, putting together a huge bonfire in the market square. But when the news of the German surrender was announced by Churchill over the radio, and later confirmed in the King's speech at nine p.m., people were slow to respond. We went to bed at our usual time, but were woken by a hammering on the door about midnight. The party was on. In our dressing gowns and slippers we joined the crowd going down the Great North Road to the blazing bonfire in the square. The Town Hall was floodlit and we laughed and danced and sang and hugged and kissed until about three a.m.

With the war in Europe over I was genuinely hopeful of a bright new, brand new morrow and applauded the Labour victory in the General Election in July 1945. Mother was furious.

"It's a disgrace to treat a man like Winston that way!" she said in one of her rare letters.

I cannot remember any celebrations when the war with Japan ended. The dropping of atom bombs seemed more like a disaster than a victory. The years 1946 and 1947 were bad for most people with increasing austerity, coal shortages and cuts in electricity. The good humoured jokes about "we can take it" became bad tempered complaints and the local traders took a lot of stick from their customers.

Tilly and Trixie were ill with a flu-like virus. Somehow I nursed them through the bitterly cold weather despite my inability to walk as far as the garden gate. Neighbours helped with the shopping but by February 1947 I was near collapse. One of the girls from the office helped me to get to Hill End Mental

Hospital in St Albans to see Dr Mannheim. I walked into his office, said "Hello" and fainted.

Dr Mannheim persuaded me to stay at the hospital for further psychotherapy. It was back to the old routine. The theory was excellent. You hunted down through the labyrinth of your past to confront and outface the devil there. And hey presto, the devil and the fear of him were gone. Great stuff if it worked, but it did not. But over those eight months I provided employment for several budding psychiatrists and became interested in painting.

The first lesson I sat through and refused to co-operate. Lesson is perhaps the wrong word. We were given large sheets of paper, poster paints, brushes and invited to paint whatever picture came into our poor addled minds. The second time, to please the teacher, a delightful man Mr Cahoon, I painted a simple stark picture of a derelict house on a deserted country road. I painted that same picture week after week. Mr Cahoon was interested in the broken roof, the empty staring windows, the bleak bare road. I became interested in colour.

I covered sheets with the house usually sombre with heavy grey or purple clouds, but at times shot through with bursts of yellow, orange, red or green. Then, purely by chance, leafing through some old magazines, I found a picture of St Clement Danes. I could not draw then and I cannot draw now. Paint went slap on to the paper, the shape lopsided, distorted, grotesque even, St Clement Danes lit by shafts of light.

159

Some of these paintings were passed on to Dr Mannheim and his merry men, all no doubt looking for phallic symbols. One of the pictures, a swirling mass of yellow, the good doctor put up in his office. Some, along with paintings by other patients, went on display in St Albans. I received two awards of merit and all my paintings were sold by auction. After leaving Hill End I did not touch a paint brush for twenty years but at least I began to examine closely any pictures I saw.

Dr Mannheim regretted that he could not rid me of my phobic condition, but suggested a clerical job with some responsibility, living in a secure environment such as a hospital. This, with occasional help from him would enable me to cope adequately with the future. Very much improved in health, I returned briefly to Trixie and Kayser Bondor. At the same time I applied for and was granted an interview for live-in receptionist with clerical experience at a government training centre in Letchworth.

The training centre was strictly functional, with workshops and rows of wooden chalets enclosed within a high wire mesh fence. It could just as easily have been a prison camp. Mr Henry, the manager, a tall heavy muscular man with a black Alsatian dog at his feet, could have been prison governor. The man and the dog were a formidable combination.

The interview was fairly long. I explained my circumstances as objectively as possible. Mr Henry phoned Kayser Bondor.

"Well, that's fine," he said, "Nothing but praise. Now the job I am offering you is similar to a hotel receptionist, but there is a lot more paper work and at times you'll have to take over the switchboard. There are approximately a thousand men trainees and twenty women."

I stood up to go.

"I'm not working with a thousand men!"

Mr Henry was amused and not displeased.

"Do sit down, Miss Parker. It is a necessary part of your job to stand no nonsense. A lot of these men are disabled like yourself. Some can't cope with civvy street and a lot of them can be awkward, but they are here to learn a trade, not for a holiday. They receive excellent counselling and advice, but that is not your job or mine. We are here to make the system work. Do you understand? Right, I'll get someone to show you around before you decide."

Standing apart from the workshops, the main building consisted of reception, offices, switchboard, a very large dining room, several lounges and quiet rooms and a large recreation hall. The recreation hall was used every night for dances or cinema shows or whist drives. All the entertainment was free. The bedrooms in separate chalets were fairly basic but each had a comfortable bed, wash bowl with hot and cold water, wardrobe and dressing table. There was a small sick bay.

All the staff, a dozen in administration, fifty instructors and another fifty domestics, all lived in the camp. It suited me just fine. Not only did I feel physically secure but I would be able to see Trixie and

Tilly regularly, enjoy the social life of Baldock, and be better off financially. I started a week later.

There were three receptionists, Zelda, Mary and myself and we worked in shifts from seven thirty a.m. to ten thirty p.m. Zelda was a beautiful myopic heavyweight from Roumania whose family, so she said, had been bankers. Her knowledge of English was limited and she was loftily indifferent to the residents, whose eyes seldom moved higher than her magnificent bosom. But she was good with the filing and in helping to sort out the virulent quarrels between members of the domestic staff, most of whom came from the Balkans.

When the shouting and the tumult reached high drama, Zelda marched out, a huge-thighed goddess, to restore order and dispense justice. In the background, standing like a block of granite with Nero at his heels, would be Mr Henry. Blessed are the peacemakers. Scowls were turned into smiles and raised fists into handshakes.

Mary was no lightweight, blonde, buxom and, from Mr Henry's viewpoint, inclined to be too friendly with the residents. We got on well enough but she was quite happy for me to take the responsibility when the going got rough.

When necessary I cheerfully worked from seven thirty a.m. to ten thirty p.m. There was always something to do. We never caught up with the backlog of amendments to rules and regulations flooding in from the Ministry on high. Those files are probably stored away to this day, unread and disregarded. I spent much of my leisure time with the refugees who were eager to learn English. With the statuesque Zelda I held unofficial, unscheduled classes with Poles, Czechs, Hungarians, Slavs, anyone who wanted to join in. The classes or meetings usually took place in the dining hall at eight-thirty in the evening over cups of tea and coffee.

"What is gor blimey, please?" and "Sod you Charlie?" These impromptu lessons were often hilarious, with one interpreter speaking for another interpreter on behalf of another. "You thick as a plank!" went round and round in circles and "Dim as a Toc H lamp" never got explained. Some of the trainees made snide remarks about my friendship with the refugees, but I told them in very basic English what they could do about it.

With every intake of trainees there were usually some members of the awkward squad and these were sent to me. My stock response was along the lines, "If you don't want to answer the questions, you don't want to be here. And if you don't want to be here, you won't be needing a bedroom key. So next one please." Finally there was always Mr Henry to take them aside for a fatherly word of advice. In the case of obvious illness or exhaustion, there was the sick bay and the local doctor.

Once again I was sitting pretty, assured at work, enjoying a full social life, money in the bank, with only bad dreams to trouble me. That was until the afternoon of 6 September 1948. In walked Francis Dallin. He was smoking a pipe and wearing an expensive leather jacket. He looked like a pilot which he was not. He looked rich which he was not. He looked intelligent and on that I make no comment.

Poets, philosophers and song-writers have all written of what is or is not love. It has taken me forty years to arrive at my own definition, "a strong biological urge strengthened by interlocking neuroses". In the best romantic tradition our eyes met and we fell in love there, instantly at that exact moment of time, and we both knew it.

It thrilled, frightened and confused me. What are you supposed to do when you are struck by lightning? I resolved to be cool, calm and efficient. The next man in, as it were, was busily undressing me with his eyes so I sent him packing with a flea in his ear. The next five I dispatched a bit smartish as well. And there he stood, the man in the leather jacket. I put on my best Bette Davis act of icy indifference.

"Name?"

"Francis Dallin." His voice reminded me of Mr Harvey of Moët and Chandon. Lightning struck in the same place twice and I forgot all about Bette Davis. I jumped a couple of questions.

"Are you married?"

"Not yet."

The next question was not even on the list.

"Engaged?"

"Not yet."

I returned to the proper business of completing the file. When I handed him his key he leant across the counter: "May I ask you a question?"

"Certainly," I replied graciously.

"What are you doing this evening?"

"I shall be minding my own business and would you mind taking your elbows off the counter!"

The mating game had begun. When he left the desk I asked one of the girls on the switchboard to take over.

"Are you all right, Ethel?"

"Yes. No. I think my knicker elastic just gave way," — which was a Freudian slip if ever there was one.

That evening at the dance I was on duty taking the tickets. I was taking my ease on a couch convenient to the door when in strolled Dallin.

"You look like the Rokeby Venus, with clothes on."

Having no idea what or who he was talking about, I told him to push off.

He returned with two cups of tea and told me to shove over. We were still talking when the housekeeper came round to lock up, and the next night, and the next night and the next. At first he only kissed my hand and left me at my chalet with "Goodnight, my love." The first kiss on my lips was not one of those crash, bang, wallop, tongue down your throat efforts, but soft, tender, gently exploratory, as were his fingers tracing my eyebrows, my cheekbones, and the outline of my lips.

When the first real kisses began I hung round his neck as if I were drowning. The more I wanted him, the more adamant became my arguments; we could not go on. I pointed out that I was thirty-seven and he only twenty-eight. He assured me that he preferred older women.

"How kind," I said somewhat taken aback. "Obviously you speak from experience."

"Well, I was a milkman before the war and" — he shrugged his shoulders — "you know how it is."

"No, I don't know how it is nor do I want to know how it was!" I flounced off. A bloody womanizing milkman! I could just imagine it. "Two pints today, madam, and was there anything else I can offer?" The smarmy sod!

The next morning at seven thirty a.m. he was leaning against the counter and I literally gave him the elbow, catching him smartly in the ribs as I pushed past. And there, where everyone could see, he pinned me against the counter, kissed me and threatened to go on kissing me until I agreed to meet him again. "Unhand me!" I demanded melodramatically and we both fell about laughing. That evening I felt torn to shreds as I explained about the war, my phobias, and my long sessions with Dr Mannheim. I even told him about Douglas.

For his part he had wanted on demob to own his own farm. He had gone about it competently enough, but kept cracking up. Finally it was found that his left kidney had been smashed by bomb blast and he had a nephrectomy. He had bouts of black depression which alcohol made worse. He had spent all his money and apart from a small pension had nothing.

I should have stopped the whole thing then and there, but having agreed that life was a tragedy we laughed immoderately at each other's stories and I felt ridiculously happy. Mother put a stop to that. In late

November I went home for the weekend and she forcibly reminded me of my disabilities. I decided it was time to come to my senses.

On returning to the hostel I kissed Francis goodbye. Bette Davis could not have done it better. Even so, I thought, he could have protested more than he did. I got ready for bed feeling really miserable. I had just got into my nightdress when cold air blew in from the window and there was Dallin climbing in over the sill.

I didn't know whether to shout for help or belt him one. Before I could make up my mind, my nightdress was on the floor and I forgot to pick it up.

I awoke next morning with a song in my heart, but still the same impregnable Miss Parker.

I examined myself critically in the mirror. There was not a part of me he had not kissed. My virginity he dismissed as a mere technicality to be resolved later. The cheek of the man to take it for granted that last night's performance was to be repeated again and perhaps again and again. Then it occurred to me that he might have changed his mind and I could not get dressed fast enough. Luck favours fools and lovers, thereby being double insured he evaded Mr Henry and Nero night after night, strolling across the green so casually, so damned slowly, I was melting inside before he got over the sill.

I cannot remember why we decided at Christmas to part for ever. We gave it the full treatment, heartfelt sighs, stricken eyes, Shakespeare's "Goodnight, goodnight, parting is such sweet sorrow" to Housman's more apt and evocative

"Shake hands, we shall never be friends, all's over;
I only vex you the more I try.
All's wrong that ever I've done or said,
And nought to help it in this dull head.
Shake hands, good luck, goodbye.
But if you came to a road where danger
Or guilt or anguish or shame's to bear,
Be good to the lad that loves you true
And the soul that was born to die for you,
And whistle and I'll be there."

He went home to Benfleet, I to Baldock. He gave me a small brooch of the Laughing Cavalier to remember him by; what I really wanted was a whistle. After carol singing with the choir on Christmas Eve, and exhorting everyone to be of good cheer, I locked myself in the loo and bawled my eyes out. All I wanted for Christmas was Francis. What did it really matter if his legs were skinny, his knees knobbly and his feet too big as long as he told me my skin was as smooth as jade, as soft as satin, and he loved me. At last I knew the certainty of being loved, of being wanted, of being prized. He made me feel uniquely feminine.

It is said there is one who loves and one who is loved. I accept that Francis desperately needed someone to love and I desperately needed to be loved, hence the interlocking neuroses, but the roles are not immutably fixed. The wonder and the beauty is that one gives what the other needs when it is needed.

Although not on duty, I returned to the hostel on Boxing Day certain he would be waiting. The swine wasn't there. That's it, I thought, damn and blast him and the Shropshire Lad and the Bard of Avon. The storeman, who I genuinely liked became alcoholically amorous and got a thick ear for his pains.

I lay awake listening to the hollow bells at midnight when my window slammed open and Francis fell into the room. It was about two hours later and we were resting when he raised his head from my belly and said:

"It's time you made an honest man of me, so I'll accept."

"You'll accept what exactly?"

"Your proposal of marriage."

Happily I banged his head against the wall.

Unfortunately we woke the girl in the next room. Wearing nothing but his trilby and shoes, Francis scrambled out of the window. I threw the rest of his clothes after him and just had time to put on my dressing gown when Elsa came in.

"I'm sorry, Elsa, I must have been dreaming."

"Oh yes, and who's out there with the bare what do you call it? Father Christmas or reindeer?"

We both looked out of the window and, oh God, he looked so funny. He turned round stark naked and started to do the Highland Fling, either that or tossing the caber. Elsa and I were convulsed. Afterwards we sat on my bed and I said:

"The fool wants me to marry him."

"Really? Will you?"

"I don't know, life is such a mess."

"You not with baby?"

"Lord no, I'm still a virgin."

I had difficulty in explaining the word virgin. Her eyes opened wide.

"He come here night after night, you make all that noise, and you still a virgin?"

I was startled.

"You knew all the time?"

"Sure, everybody know, you think we all as thick as plank?"

Elsa exaggerated, not everyone knew. I was now so deeply in love, I did not care anyway. I was not playing games any more. Even if it meant losing him, Francis had to understand the extent of my disabilities. I insisted we sought the opinion of Dr Mannheim and Francis reluctantly agreed.

My continued virginity also bothered me, but he refused to do anything about that.

"It will sort itself out at the proper time, believe me."

"Bloody Mr Know All," I said, pulling his head down to my breasts.

We had to wait a few weeks to see Mannheim, but drunk with happiness and blessed by unusually good weather we spent our spare time wandering the streets of London. I bought a superb coat at Derry and Toms. Then by chance we came upon the Bayeux Tapestry, on exhibition for the first time in this country. It was also the first time I had been in a museum or gallery and I was entranced.

Afterwards we had an expensive tea in some little posh restaurant. We were both dressed up to the nines. Francis had very good clothes at that time. A superior young man remarked to his companion: "Parvenus."

That meant nothing to me, but as we went out, Francis bent over the very large young man:

"We ain't parvenus, mate, we're boracic, so watch yer norf and sarf, or I'll push that jam tart up yer hooter."

The young man gawped. I pulled Francis into the street.

"What's a parvenu, you fool?"

"A mongrel with money."

"And what's boracic?"

"Boracic lint, skint."

"So what does that make us?"

"A couple of mongrels without money." We went on our way singing "We ain't got a barrel of money, we may be ragged and funny, but we travel along singing a song side by side."

We did not make a habit of that sort of thing. At a later date we went to the Wallace Collection to see the Laughing Cavalier, but I was more interested in the Sèvres porcelain. On another day to the National Gallery to see the Rokeby Venus.

"My bum's not that big!" I protested.

"No but it's the same lovely shape though."

On yet another day we went to the Tate. Francis went to an attendant and spoke to him quietly. Returning, he took my hand and asked me to close my eyes. I followed them until he said: "Open your eyes and take a butcher's." I opened my eyes to the colour, the burst of genius that is Turner. I felt a shiver of excitement from the roots of my hair down to my toenails. He must have been a very passionate man, there is sexual energy in those explosions of paint. To me Turner is the greatest painter of all time. On impulse I kissed first Francis and then the attendant full on the lips. The latter said:

"Blimey, we've got lots more in the basement!"

The interview with Dr Mannheim was cordial but brief.

"I have never seen you look so well, Ethel." He refused to see Francis on his own.

"I saw you both coming into the hospital. That young man is so in love with you. I could only tell him the truth, and the truth is that you are an intelligent and capable woman and he should marry you as soon as possible."

At the door of his office he shook hands with us both, wished us good luck and goodbye.

The next two months were strange ones. Those friends who had been at first congratulatory about my relationship with Francis began to urge caution. As Trixie pointed out, he had no money and no real prospects. The other problem was his inability to socialize. He suffered from people sickness and it showed. Small talk he had none, until the evening when Katie Steinfeld showed up. He was immediately all attention and in two minutes flat they were closeted together on the far side of the room.

She flirted with him outrageously, from the coy young Juliet, to the haughty Katharine and then to mature, sultry Cleopatra, showing just a suggestion of remarkably well-rounded thigh. He sat there like a country bumpkin, lapping it up, his eyes shining with admiration. People began to take notice. There were knowing smiles and polite asides of how well they were getting on together.

"I'll kill him," I thought. "I'll kill them both." When I composed myself to look again they were even closer together with her hand on his knee. Katie looked up as I approached.

"Ah, Ethel, I am trying to persuade Francis to act in our *Pygmalion*. With his splendid voice he would make an ideal Professor Higgins."

With an effort of restraint that nearly choked me, I stopped myself from saying that without his trousers he would make the ideal rear end of a camel. I said:

"So good to see you looking well, Katie, wish there was time to chat but we must be going."

Katie turned to Francis: "I must see you again soon."

"Indeed," said Francis. Not Pygmalion likely, I thought.

In the taxi back to the hostel I cut into his tiresome repetition of Katie's sterling quotations with:

"Next weekend we should go and see your parents and my mother."

"Why is that?"

"To tell them we are getting married, of course."

He looked out of the window of the taxi and I wondered what excuse he would make. He took my ringless hand in his hand. "Isn't there —" he hesitated, "Isn't there such a thing as a special licence so that we can cut out the waffle and the waiting?"

I closed my eyes and said a short penance: "Father, forgive me for I have sinned."

I expected trouble from Mother, of course. We arrived in time for dinner and she watched dourly as Francis ate her burnt offering. Her only comment to me was an enigmatic "You should know something about men by now" and "You had better arrange it with the vicar of St Thomas's about the licence."

We had tea at Benfleet. Francis's parents seemed to accept our plans with equanimity and assured us we would always be welcome there. The only other relative for whom Francis had any affection was a well-to-do aunt with property in and around London and we went to stay with her on the following weekend. She was quite, quite charming. We went to see *Bless the Bride* at the Adelphi, a happy augury indeed.

When she and I were alone she amiably asked what plans had we for the future. She found my answer "To get married as soon as possible" somewhat short of substance. She mentioned a comfortable bungalow and garden nursery at Ruislip. Did I think this would be suitable for Francis and myself?

That same weekend she took me over a fully furnished flat. Did I like it? She also showed me a crescent of converted mews.

"I own all these. They are very comfortable inside. Would one of these do?"

I was stunned by this abundance of riches.

"Have you spoken to Francis about this?" I asked.

"No."

She regarded me thoughtfully.

"Perhaps it might be better if you talked to him first after you've thought about it."

174

We had a carriage to ourselves on the train back to Letchworth. Between kisses I poured out my good news.

"She's fantastic," I said. "It's a wonderful gesture."

Francis kissed my eyes, my nose, my mouth and anything else available.

"And that's what it will be, a wonderful gesture. I have great affection for her. She is an exceptional woman. When I was a kid she took me to all the galleries and museums. She has a wonderful eye, but she measures art not in beauty but in pounds, shillings and pence. Everything for her has a price and that includes people. But we're not for sale, my dear, we are not for sale. For hire perhaps, but not for sale."

Nothing more was said by anyone of the bungalow, the flat or the mews. We were married by special licence at St Thomas's Church, Dagenham, on Saturday, 16 April 1949. It was a warm and sunny day. The weather helped to compensate for the perfunctory ceremony and the paucity of the reception, for rationing was still on and we could not afford to buy on the black market.

Neither Francis's father nor his aunt attended. His mother seemed mildly anxious, my mother had a look of sardonic disbelief. We went with Francis's mother down to Benfleet where all my clothes and personal effects had been sent from Letchworth. We had both assumed we would be living at Benfleet, which Francis regarded very much as home. His father made it plain that our assumption was ill-founded, we were not welcome.

We spent the Sunday walking up and down Southend Pier.

"Neurotics are supposed to be at their best in a crisis," said Francis, "but I feel curiously uninspired. How about you?"

"Well, we could jump off the end of the pier, but I don't want to die a virgin."

CHAPTER
SEVEN

Return to Dagenham

On the Monday Francis left me at Dagenham and went on to the City to get a job. He had a green card issued to disabled people by the Ministry to help them to get employment, but from bitter experience he had found the card more of a hindrance than a help.

I asked Mother whether we could store our clothes temporarily with her. She sniffed. "So this place is good enough to use as a store, but not good enough to live in I suppose, you and your clever sod of a husband."

I took a deep breath. "Are you saying we can live here?"

"As long as you pay your share."

I hugged and kissed her.

"No need to go bloody mad," she said: "and you can make a pot of tea while you're at it."

Francis came home with a job under his belt and found me busily rearranging the back room.

Mother looked at him defiantly.

"Well?" she demanded.

"Very well indeed," said Francis and kissed her hand.

With a small bed sent up from Benfleet, two armchairs I had bought before the war and a few orange boxes, we set up home. I calculated that with the wages from Francis and our two war pensions, we could manage fairly comfortably. It never occurred to either of us that I should go out to work as well. That Sunday night when I was melting, flowing, he entered into me slowly, gently. I reached down, grasped his buttocks and thrust him home. We lay a long time without moving; the rest is silence.

Later on Francis asked: "Are you all right, Mrs Dallin?"

"Never better, Mr Dallin," I replied. "There's only one thing wrong?"

"Wrong?" he sat up abruptly and peered at my face in the moonlight. "What is wrong?"

"I forgot to include the price of condoms in my budget!" With a gust of laughter he took me in his arms again and the second time was even more wonderful than the first.

Next morning he brought me a cup of tea in bed. While he shaved I cooked breakfast for all of us. Even Bill seemed pleased by the new arrangement. When the men had gone to work Mother made herself comfortable with the newspaper while I happily scrubbed, polished, mended and made do. I soon took over the entire household budget and all the cookery.

Unlike the proverbial suburban housewife, I had no time to be intimate with the milkman, although I did get rather matey with the baker. My husband, how good that sounds, my husband was actually jealous! My husband, there I've said it again, whose philosophy was "money is not worth quarrelling about and sex is too important to quarrel about" got quite ratty about the baker, and the fishmonger as well if I remember aright.

That first year was not easy. Francis had to come to terms with being a shiny-arsed clerk and, most difficult of all, to understand that not even his love could prevent the fear that paralysed me from time to time. I in turn had to cope with his black moods of depression and rage. It took some time for the neuroses to be fully locked. Which brings me to the biological urge.

We were only three months married and I had a deep hunger inside me to bear a child. Francis was troubled at first but as I pointed out:

"Think of the money we'll save on condoms!"

"You lovely, lovely fool," he said and our love-making took on a new urgency and delight. And nothing happened. I, who for years had remained a virgin for fear of pregnancy, could not conceive.

I consulted with two neighbours who had become friends and was confounded by their ignorance and prudery. Both had borne children but claimed never to have had an orgasm. One proudly boasted that her husband had never seen her naked. After some time Francis and I went to see our family doctor, the sort that doesn't exist any more, and he gave me a letter for the Fertility Clinic in Soho. I persuaded one of my neighbours to go with me to the Clinic.

Fortunately she was not present when I and another forty frustrated would-be mums were sitting shoulder to shoulder in a corridor waiting to see the gynaecologist. A junior male doctor with the voice of a sergeant-major on parade, asked the preliminary questions — name, address, frequency of intercourse and so on. The answers did not come trippingly off the tongue for some.

"Twice," was the first quietly confidential reply.

"Twice what?" boomed the young man.

"Er, twice a week," was the bashful reply.

"Orgasm?"

"Sometimes."

I listened with increasing incredulity. Twice a week seemed to be at the top of the scale. I was offended by the lack of privacy. Should I tell the truth? The young man began his inquisition. I stood up, took his clipboard and pen from him and filled in the necessary details. I pushed the clipboard under his nose.

"And that young man, is strictly confidential. Do you understand?" I complained to the senior doctor that the procedure in the corridor was degrading to women. She readily agreed and asked me whether I could put that in writing. "You're damned right I can," and it gave me some pleasure to do so.

After several visits, including one carrying a sample of sperm from Francis in a tube cocooned in cotton wool to keep it warm, I had my fallopian tubes cleared. By a happy coincidence this was at the time of our first wedding anniversary. Because our vows had taken a bruising during those first few months we decided to renew them.

The vicar was surprised and moved by our request. In an empty church but for the vicar, the organist and ourselves, we solemnly re-affirmed our love and our vows till death us do part. The vicar said he felt privileged to have conducted the service and he and the organist wished us well.

We went home to our small room, and with candles on the top of orange boxes, we had a wedding feast of cold partridge and wine. It is possible that that night our daughter was conceived. She was born on 30 January 1951.

Mother refused to believe that I had become pregnant by intent, so I explained about the Soho Clinic and my fallopian tubes.

"Flopping tubes, flopping tubes! Trust you to have flopping tubes! I've never heard the like."

Finally starting from first principles I gave her a basic lesson, complete with illustrations, on the mechanics of conception. "You don't have to tell me where his cock goes," she said contemptuously, but she was interested. When her friends came to tea I could hear her giving a progress report. She was now *the* expert on all matters pertaining to the uterus, fallopian tubes and ovaries. There was a hush whenever I entered her room and several pairs of knowing, elderly eyes watched my behaviour and considered my shape.

"She looks well enough at the moment," I heard one of them say grudgingly, "But it's early days yet." There followed a long discussion about miscarriages, breach births and so on.

I joyfully ignored all their prognostications of woe, for never had I felt so well, so happy or so hungry. In between, during and after meals I comforted myself with fresh pineapples and stayed myself with flagons of milk. However, for every plus there is usually a minus. I

181

paid for that carefree gestation with a long and painful delivery.

Part of the problem was my inability to bend my injured leg. My mind went into a time warp to the operation without anaesthetic in Botleys. I sweated and pushed to no avail. They were preparing me for a Caesarean when I gave one more almighty shove and my daughter began to move. When she finally emerged I was exhausted but triumphant — I had done it!

During the next few months while I breast fed our daughter, Francis was forever reading books like *The Intelligent Parents' Guide*. I listened, loved the silly man and went on doing what came naturally.

Mother criticized everything of course and often provoked me to tears, tears of anger. The next five years passed pleasantly enough. Francis was earning more money as the manager of a small office for a local firm. We spent too many weekends at Benfleet for my liking but to compensate we also explored London, its parks, galleries and museums which were all free.

The best way to see London then was from the top of a bus and for a total of twelve shillings and sixpence on Red Rover tickets, a packet of sandwiches and a flask of tea we were able to get as far as Hampton Court or Windsor. Sometimes we went to the People's Palace at Poplar, or the Theatre Royal at Stratford, but when really flush we went to good old Drury Lane.

During 1955 Mother had a number of serious illnesses and had reason to be satisfied with her choice of son-in-law. He often sat with her all night while I slept fitfully, fully clothed on a chair in the other room.

We were both haggard by the time she came back from that undiscovered country from which no traveller was supposed to return. Her first demands were always for a pot of tea and her insurance policies. Dr Holmstead, wonderful man, was greeted by his ungrateful patient with "You thought I'd gone that time!"

Bill's contribution at these times, "She should be put away," was dismissed with angry contempt. But that is what happened.

In 1956, just as our daughter started school, I recovered from an unpleasant bout of pneumonia to receive confirmation that I had a malignant tumour in my left breast. At that time I knew little about cancer or its consequences. I told Mother nothing but it was arranged for a hospital visitor to see her and suggest she went away for a rest. Not only did she agree but said she would be only too glad to get away from her selfish bitch of a daughter. I sat sick at heart, while accused of everything short of matricide.

"What about your son-in-law?"

"Oh, he's as soft as shit."

Miserably I walked the visitor to the gate.

"It isn't really like that," I said.

"I know, my dear," she patted my hand, "I accept Dr Holmstead's report and trust all will go well with you."

So our daughter went to Benfleet, my Mother to one hospital and I to another. After the mastectomy I had a month's radiotherapy. The radiation room was large with thick leadlined walls and ceiling. The parts of my body not subject to radiation were covered by sandbags and although I could see the faces of the radiologists through a small window I felt trapped, alone, waiting for the ceiling to fall in. At the end of it all I felt as limp as a rag doll, but Francis held me as if I were a fragile precious work of art. A work of art! With one tit missing and part of one thigh gone, I looked like a Piccaso after a pissup!

However, as I grew stronger, Mother became weaker. Our daughter was able to come home, but not Mother. We used to visit her three times a week. She had almost given up. She wanted to die, to die at home but I said nothing, my care was for my child. She looked at me with those tired, shrewd old eyes and read my mind. But she was not quite done for yet. There was still good old "soft as shit" Francis.

"Frank," she pleaded, "Frank, please take me home."

He stroked her thin hands and arms.

"I'll try, Emily, by Christ I'll try."

We walked in silence from the hospital. I expected him to be angry, his usual reaction to events beyond his control. He was surprisingly matter of fact.

"She's coming home even if I pack in my job and nurse her myself. Do you understand?"

"Of course, my love. But there's no need to give up your job. We'll manage it together as we've always done." And I meant it, but Emily died in her sleep next morning in that dreadful hospital on 28 January, 1957.

We could not afford any fine horse-drawn hearse for Emily. The funeral was the cheapest I could arrange. Those precious insurance policies met only a fraction of the cost and Bill's contribution was negligible.

I did not weep as the coffin was lowered into the grave. "Free at last" I thought.

How mother would have laughed at that!

At least I got rid of Bill. I found him comfortable lodgings, packed his bags, wished him good luck, goodbye and good riddance.

Unfortunately I could not rid myself of the panic attacks which followed no predictable pattern. Nor could Francis get rid of his detestation of Dagenham and clerical work. We survived some very bad times, holding to each other like the lost Babes in the Wood. I had to pay for my trouble-free years of menstruation with a severe menopausal depression made worse by a chronic pain in my lower back. All the time that I had been walking with no outward sign of injury other than, as Francis put it, a sexy tilt of the hips, the disc between the fourth and fifth vertebrae was being eroded. I collapsed in spectacular fashion, the X-rays showing that the bones themselves were rubbing together. I had to have six months complete bedrest and then had to wear a surgical corset and surgical shoes.

It was about this time we met Jimmy. He was a short, shabby, funny little man. A gifted amateur painter and a collector of objets d'art in jade, ivory, gold and silver. Ours was a curious relationship, not platonic but not sexual either, not as I understand it anyway. Although older than I, he was no father figure. If anything I was the mother figure. He loved to be cuddled and told what a clever boy he was. He told me again and again how he had made his fortune on the Stock Exchange.

As he often helped me in and out of bed he saw rather a lot of me, in more ways than one, and made some flattering sketches of me in the nude. But one sketch, drawn in ink on brown paper, of me as I really was, a tired middle aged woman with a mastectomy, made the others look trivial, as indeed they were. But in this one I was so truly naked, so open, so vulnerable, I was reluctant for Francis to see it and Jimmy seemed a little embarrassed. But Francis kissed me, "This is really good. We must keep this one."

When I was able to get up and about, Jimmy gave me a present of some beautiful sable brushes and taught me to paint in oils. We spent many affectionate happy hours together. I usually painted the conventional landscape or still life, but sometimes in the middle of the night, driven by pain, I created bizarre scenes of blue suns, green skies, crimson fields shot with vivid splashes of yellow and orange. Francis thought they were terrific, Jimmy hated them, but every one of them sold, not for much it is true, but they sold.

Then Jimmy went and buggered up the whole cosy arrangement. He arrived one morning to take me to a private gallery in the West End. He was superbly suited, handsomely groomed and we travelled in style by taxi. We first made a call at his bank, to be greeted with due deferences by the manager. At the gallery I was surprised to be introduced first to one artist and then another.

One little horror even shorter than Jimmy pursued me round the gallery. He was an abstract painter, a painter of ideas but his conversation was very much of country matters and I told him to piss off. I was not impressed by any of the paintings or the artists and was glad to get away.

From there Jimmy and I went to Simpson's in the Strand. We were shown straight to our table with the same deference Jimmy had enjoyed at the bank. Everything about Simpson's was superb, the decor, the service, the food. This was luxury, this was living.

After coffee Jimmy took my hand, "Ethel," he said, "Will you come away with me?"

I thought of Emily and nearly replied, "Not if your arse was hung with diamonds, mate." Instead, I asked for time to think. Safely back home I said that the most offensive thing about his invitation was his betrayal of Francis. And that was the end of that artistic episode.

Our daughter was at university when I became so disabled that Francis, with the help of another splendid doctor, Patrick Briggs, took the difficult decision to give up work to look after me. He was very close to a breakdown himself by then. The next nineteen years we have never been out of each other's company except for the times I spent in hospital or when I went out driving. At the age of sixty I passed my driving test in a specially adapted mini. I never went far but even going to the doctor on my own was an adventure.

It was going to the doctor on my seventieth birthday for a routine examination in order to renew my car insurance that brought my driving to an end. A lump on the old mastectomy scar proved to be malignant. The operation was unpleasant and the radiation afterwards scarred my lung.

The past few years have gone by quickly. We read a lot together, especially poetry of the Thirties — that old gang of Auden, Spender, Day Lewis and Mac Neice. But now that the secondary cancer has entered me more intimately than any lover, getting into my very bones, two lines of Eliot come constantly to mind:

"And I have seen the eternal Footman hold my
    coat and snicker,
And in short, I was afraid."

I am afraid now. Kind and caring though the staff at the hospice are, I do not want to die there. I want to die at home in my husband's arms.

I am sure Emily would not laugh at that.

Postscript

Ethel died in St Francis Hospice, Havering, on Monday 24th June 1991, five weeks short of her eightieth birthday.

The joy and reward of loving that brave lady, the richness of that reward does not console me for her loss.

It is not so much pain I feel as a sort of emptiness. Part of me is missing, the best part, the part that was Ethel.

Francis Dallin

ISIS publish a wide range of books in large print, from fiction to biography. Any suggestions for books you would like to see in large print or audio are always welcome. Please send to the Editorial department at:

ISIS Publishing Ltd.
7 Centremead
Osney Mead
Oxford OX2 0ES
(01865) 250 333

A full list of titles is available free of charge from:
Ulverscroft large print books

(UK)
The Green
Bradgate Road, Anstey
Leicester LE7 7FU
Tel: (0116) 236 4325

(Australia)
P.O Box 953
Crows Nest
NSW 1585
Tel: (02) 9436 2622

(USA)
1881 Ridge Road
P.O Box 1230, West Seneca,
N.Y. 14224-1230
Tel: (716) 674 4270

(Canada)
P.O Box 80038
Burlington
Ontario L7L 6B1
Tel: (905) 637 8734

(New Zealand)
P.O Box 456
Feilding
Tel: (06) 323 6828

Details of **ISIS** complete and unabridged audio books are also available from these offices. Alternatively, contact your local library for details of their collection of **ISIS** large print and unabridged audio books.